JUMPSTART

YOUR MARRIAGE

& YOUR MONEY

ELLE MARTINEZ

ISBN: 0998805157
ISBN-13: 978-0998805153

*To my family and friends, I'm so grateful for
your love and support.*

CONTENTS

INTRODUCTION

L et me be upfront, money is not the most important thing in life, but it can be a huge source of frustration, stress, and tension in a marriage. In fact, a survey by Sun-Trust Bank found that 35 percent of married couples cite money as the leading issue they fight about. But as someone who interviews married couples about their finances, I have yet to meet a couple who wanted to intentionally sabotage their marriage.

Time and again, I have found that marriages are nearly destroyed by not talking about money (because spouses want to avoid a fight), not having a financial plan, and not having a clear idea of how they're spending money as a couple.

The good news is that money doesn't have to be a weight on your marriage any longer. Instead, you can learn how to use it to build a life that you will love. The sooner that you can get comfortable managing and discussing your finances as a couple, the less stress and more fun you'll have together.

Whether you're newlyweds or have been married for years, I'll take you through a process that will jumpstart your marriage and money in just four weeks. By the end, you'll have all the tools you need to manage your money and take charge of your financial life.

Why Me?

I'm Elle Martinez, creator of *Couple Money*, a personal finance site and podcast dedicated to helping spouses work together to build wealth.

I started my site several years ago because, at the time, I couldn't find a resource that addressed the unique and sometimes difficult conversations that come up when discussing money and marriage. The topics I was interested in were:

• How to combine finances after saying "I do."
• How to create a joint budget.
• How to deal with (and dump) debt as a couple.
• How to approach lending money to family members.

After I got engaged, my fiancé and I decided to do the responsible thing and have "the money talk." We knew how disagreements over money could potentially ruin a marriage, so we were going to rip off the Band-Aid and put all the numbers out there in the open.

Are you cringing? Yeah, you should be, because it didn't go the way either of us expected. It turns out that he had one semester's worth of student loans and I had the trifecta of debt—credit cards, student loans, and a car loan. I couldn't even give him an exact number of how much money I actually owed!

Although it was a bit of a mess at first, we did manage to turn things around considerably. We paid off $35,000 of debt, we learned how to make saving money a routine habit, and we simplified our finances and our lives so that we have more time for the people and projects that we love.

As I began sharing our story on my site, readers chimed in with their unique experiences and a community was born. (Visit www.CoupleMoney.com for bonus material and supplemental information to accompany this book.) Soon after, I launched *The Couple Money Podcast* as a way to track the patterns displayed by successful couples who have done extraordinary things like pay off massive amounts of debt, start their own business, travel the world, and even retire early.

Understanding How "Personal" Finance Can Be

Being wealthy means something different to every couple. I believe a rich life is separate from how much money is in your bank account. Taking care of your finances, however, is an important element of marriage because it puts you in a position to give your time and money to the people and projects that matter most to you.

Remember, this is *your marriage* and *your money*.

While you need to stay on top of your money, you don't need to obsess over every penny. I'll help you strike a healthy balance by sharing tools and apps that will help alleviate the tedious parts of the process so you can focus on what really matters.

How This Book Is Designed

I love to read, but I hate personal finance books that only go over theory and provide no value in the real world. That's why I wrote this book with practical applications in mind that are designed to ensure your hard-earned money is going towards the goals that matter most to you.

I've also included a number of talking points, checklists, and activities to help you get more comfortable with money. Think of this book as a travel guide. There's going to be plenty of information about the destination you're going to visit, the foods you should try, and the sights you should see, but for it to be truly useful, you're going to have to actually go there and experience it for yourself.

Jumpstart Your Finances in Four Weeks

This book is designed to help you jumpstart your money and marriage over the course of a month. In the first week, we will look at what it is that you want to achieve with your money, and I'll help you get a clear idea of what your finances look like now. In the second week, we'll create a plan that allows you to quickly and easily manage your money and stay on top of your finances. In the third week, I'll show you how to generate additional income and save more money so you can achieve your goals faster. Finally, in the fourth week, I'll help you put together everything that you learned so you can finally achieve your goals and live a simpler, more stress-free life.

I want you to know upfront that it's okay to make mistakes. Just as your marriage will strengthen over the years as your lives merge together, your finances will improve, too. So don't worry about getting everything exactly right the first time you try. Having been there, I know that sometimes things can get heated, arguments ensue, and the best laid plans can fail. I'll help you make adjustments and diffuse tense situations as they arise. My goal is to teach you how to encourage each other so that you can have fun while building your wealth and your marriage.

WEEK 1

Creating Your Roadmap

CHAPTER 1

———•◦•———

Creating Your Dream Together

We often spend more time planning our vacations than we do our finances. Think about all of the effort that you put into planning a fantastic getaway. You research your travel destination and make a list of the must-see spots and activities. You hunt for travel deals, make reservations, and perhaps buy travel insurance. Before you've even arrived, you've already started daydreaming and have a clear picture of what your vacation will look like.

When it comes to defining your personal finance goals, however, it's unlikely that you've planned for them in as vivid detail. But the good news is that mastering your money can be as easy as planning a trip together. The first step? Defining where you want to go and why.

What Are You Trying to Achieve?

Before going on a trip, you need to know two critical pieces of information: Your starting point and your final destination.

The same is true when it comes to planning your financial goals, but for some reason we seem to have difficulty defining these two elements. And when it comes to defining your goals *as a couple*, it becomes even more difficult. Let's take the goal of retirement for example.

You may both want to retire early, but the idea of retirement may be completely different for each of you. One of you might picture being in your forever home (a cabin in the woods where you write your beloved novel) while the other is looking forward to backpacking around the world and living a more active lifestyle.

And that's normal.

Yes, the two of you have taken a vow and you're a team, but you're still you. Your personality, quirks, and dreams are yours. The exciting part is seeing how you can combine these traits with your spouse's and create a life together.

The first step to defining your retirement goal is discussing your "what" and your "why." It's important for each of you to say out loud what it is that you want to do with your money and your time during retirement. Remember, it's like planning a trip. You may have different destinations in mind at the start, but knowing what each of you wants will allow you to work together to see if a third location will make both of you happy.

The Power of Two

"Obsession" isn't usually a good term, but if you and your spouse have found your "why," it's going to be a big help. Financial guru Dave Ramsey likes to talk about having gazelle-like intensity in life. It's an idea that came from watching a documentary about a cheetah and a gazelle.

The cheetah is the fastest land mammal alive, yet when it's chasing a gazelle, it hardly ever catches it. Why?

As you can imagine, a gazelle at that point is only thinking about one thing—surviving. Dave encourages his audience to have that same intensity when it comes to paying off their debts (which we'll get to later), but I want to apply that principle to achieving all of your financial goals in general.

Without understanding your "why" and making it as real as possible, you're more than likely not going to finish this book and you're certainly not going to achieve your goals. I want you to succeed. I want to meet you in a few years and see your smiles as you tell me you're closer to achieving your dreams. Of course, that means putting in real effort, and I'm going to share with you a fantastic and fun way that you can get on the same team.

Planning Gives You Options

The purpose of this chapter is not to lock you into a single plan for the rest of your life. I understand how quickly life can change. Instead, I'd like for you to begin planning for your future with the understanding that changes will be needed. To return to our trip analogy, suppose you originally wanted to visit Paris, but now you've decided that Copenhagen would be a better destination. Great! Having saved enough money for your trip already, you can easily make that change. The important thing is to get started today and not postpone planning for your future any longer.

Mastering Money Dates

One of the easiest ways that you and your spouse can connect with your finances—while having fun—is by scheduling regular "money dates."

No, these dates aren't just about pulling out a spreadsheet and running through numbers. (What could be more romantic?) Instead, they're about making sure that your money is working towards what's important to you as a couple. These dates serve as "check-ins" and allow you to take the time to see what's working and what's not.

A money date is not the time or place to start playing the blame game or beat yourself up for past mistakes. Your conversations should instead be about encouraging each other and brainstorming solutions for any bumps in the road that you may be experiencing.

. . . .

Over the course of the first two weeks, I'll be walking you through four different money dates. These dates are designed to help get your financial plan up and running. After the fourth date, you can decide as a couple how often you'd like meet.

. . . .

Making the Most of Your Money Dates

Remember all of the fun times you had on dates before you were married? I want you to still do that. Go out and enjoy a movie, spend time together, and have a little wine (or beer if you like to homebrew). The only difference is that I want you to spend about fifteen minutes discussing your finances, too.

Before I review the process of creating your money goals together, let me offer some suggestions to make your money dates more relaxing and enjoyable.

Grab your numbers before the date. Take a bit of time to collect your numbers and have them available to both of you. If you're alarmed about how much debt you're in or how much your spouse is spending, don't unload! Instead, write down how you feel and wait until the date. Remember, these dates are to work on your financial plan together.

Make it special (not expensive). The location isn't important, but the tone is crucial. You want to be relaxed and in a good mood before you chat. For some dates, it's best to go out and mix things up. Other nights, stay in and open a bottle of wine. Your dates should make you happy.

Lay out a few ground rules. Even though you may be going over your finances and your budget, your date should be a positive experience. If there's a sensitive topic that you would like to discuss, consider setting a rule that you'll bring it up to get some initial ideas, but you'll wait a bit to work out a final solution that you both agree with.

Money Date Checklist

Because the concept of a "money date" is probably new to you, let me give you a general overview of ours. As with everything, you can modify it to fit your style.

Celebrate your wins. We like to start things off with reviewing our recent wins. It can be personal, financial, or professional. It's an opportunity to cheer each other on and set a positive vibe for the date.

Review your goals. We typically have a few short-term goals for the year (house projects, trips, helping loved ones) and some long-term plans like being financially independent by age 45. Reviewing our goals keeps our "why" in front of us all the time.

Review the numbers. Once we have an idea of where we're going, we'll then take a few minutes to review the numbers. If you're a fan of spreadsheets, this is the perfect time to pull them out. For us, we find that using tools like Personal Capital makes things a breeze. (It's also free, which makes it a double win in my book!)

Deal with hiccups. Bumps in the road are expected. That's completely normal. When they happen, we adjust deadlines, and if necessary, change our goals. While it's not a cure-all, problems become less stressful because we're working through them together. I've heard from so many couples (and we may be guilty of this ourselves) that making assumptions and not keeping each other in the loop created unnecessary headaches that could have been easily avoided.

Plan for next month. Every month seems to have its own unique projects and/or expenses associated with it, so planning ahead keeps us on target.

Enjoy the rest of your date. All work and no play isn't fun. We make sure to relax and enjoy our date!

As you can see, it's not complicated, and the finances are just a small part of the date. The key is for you and your spouse to get on the same page with your goals and make sure that your budget is working.

When we first started having money dates, we spent a lot of time chatting about our finances because we were still finding our rhythm. Over the years, though, reviewing our financial picture has become quicker and easier.

Are you feeling ready? Let's test drive your first money date!

Money Date #1: Define Your Goals & Your "Why"

Your first money date will be different from the others because you won't actually be looking at your financials.

Instead, the two of you are going to have some fun together and figure out which goals are important to you and why.

Celebrate Your Wins

You might feel like there are no financial wins to celebrate yet, but the fact that you're doing this is a win for your relationship and is setting you on the path to financial success. That's worth celebrating!

Review Your Goals

So, here's where you'll be spending most of your time during your first money date—figuring out what you want to do with your money.

Let's start with your why.

If you didn't have to worry about money, what would you want to do with your life? Take a few minutes and visualize it. Where are you? What are you doing? What does your "typical" day look like? Write it down and share it with your spouse.

Once you've discussed what your lives would look like if money was not a concern, take some time to find the common ground that you're both fired up over. (Think of the gazelle and the cheetah. What could the two of you pursue with that same passion?) Once you come together on what it is that you want your future to look like, you can truly be a dynamic duo. (No offense Batman and Robin.)

Now that you've set your long-term retirement goal, come up with three milestones that can help you get there. Focus on something that you can accomplish over the next six months, one year, and five years. Why the staggered plan? Because I want you to enjoy some early wins to start building momentum as a team.

Review the Numbers

It's now time to attribute dollar values to your retirement goal and the three milestones that you've determined. For example:

- **Long-term goal: Financially independent by age 45.**
Amount: $1,000,000; the amount needed to cover essential expenses during retirement.

- **Six-month milestone: Pay off credit cards.**
Amount: $1,500; the balance owed on your credit cards.

- **One-year milestone: Start a sustainable side business.**
Amount: $1,000 per month; the amount that you consistently want to earn each month from your business.

- **Five-year milestone: Quit office jobs by age 40.**
Amount: $150,000; the amount needed, in addition to your retirement savings, to cover expenses for transitional years as you build your side business.

At this point, during your first money date, it's not important to worry about the "how" or pinpointing exact numbers. We'll review and refine those later. All I want you to do today is start dreaming and planning together. Jot down your goals and keep them in a safe spot where you can see them, and always start your future money dates by reviewing them.

Deal With Hiccups

Life happens, so take a minute and look for potential snags that need to be straightened out before your next money date. Don't be discouraged by these, but instead use them as motivation to come together as a team and work through them.

Plan for Next Month

Are there any large expenses that you expect to incur over the next month? Talking about them now will remind you to put them in your budget and begin planning for them in the weeks ahead.

Enjoy the Rest of Your Date!

You did it! You've completed your first money date; how does it feel? Do you have a better sense of where you're heading? Are you more hopeful knowing that you have goals you're that working on together? Good! Now go finish the rest of your date and relax!

———•••———

Overcoming Obstacles When Setting Goals

If setting goals with your spouse didn't go as smoothly as you would have liked, don't be discouraged! In fact, it's not surprising if you're not immediately on the same page, considering you're individuals with your own dreams and ambitions.

Let's work through a common scenario together; one in which you are looking forward to starting a business and your spouse is interested in investing more money for retirement. This is where you're going to have to step back and find a single goal that you can agree on, and build from there.

Keeping with this example, if you'd like to start your own business, it would be wise to optimize your monthly spending. Maybe it's not the long-term goal that you had in mind, or the "why" that motivates you every day, but it's a great foundation for you and your spouse to start working together.

You can then break down your goal of optimizing your monthly spending by adding smaller milestones like creating a comprehensive budget and cutting frivolous expenses. With the money that you've saved, you can use part of it as seed money for your new business (your goal), and part of it to put towards retirement contributions (your spouse's goal).

A First-Timers Guide to Setting Goals

Rather than having different opinions about what your goals should be, maybe you're having trouble setting goals in general. You may be having difficulty finding your "why," and that's very common. If you find yourself in this position, my best advice is simple: Avoid the word "goals."

Wait, hear me out.

People hear the word "goals" and they tense up. They conjure images of classroom essays and job interviews. Goals sound and feel big, weighty, and overwhelming.

Instead, I want you to brainstorm what you want to do, where you want to go, and who you want to be. Start by asking yourselves these questions:

- If you didn't have to earn money, how would you spend your time?
- Would you like to buy a home? Where?
- Would you like to travel around the world? Would you prefer mini-vacations or a long, extended trip?
- Are you interested in starting a family? How many kids?
- Do you want to start your own business? What hobbies do you have that you could turn into a business?
- Would you like to volunteer? Start a charity? If money was not a concern, what charities would you support?

Now that you've asked these questions and considered your answers, let's go one step further. Now ask, "Why?" for each of them.

This question not only gives you a better idea of what it is that you really want, but it makes it easier for the two of you to find common goals that you can build on.

- Why do you want to travel?
- Why do you want to start a business?
- Why do you want to volunteer?

Open and Honest Communication is Key

The success of a financial plan, and to a certain extent a marriage, boils down to keeping the lines of communication open and making tough discussions as positive as possible. Without these factors, you may find yourself withholding valuable information and distancing yourself from your spouse. That's why I love money dates—they encourage open communication as a way to bring you closer together, achieve your dreams, and protect yourselves from the unknown.

Some couples mistakenly believe that if they ignore a certain topic, they'll avoid money arguments and their marriage will be healthier. That's simply not true. Instead, it's the lack of meaningful communication between spouses that leads to arguments in the first place.

To initiate the more difficult or sensitive conversations about money, I suggest following these guidelines:

Pick the right time to talk. Having an in-depth financial conversation the moment your spouse walks through the door is not ideal. Also avoid conversations about money during each other's personal time, like when your spouse is catching up on his or her favorite TV show.

Introduce your concern with politeness and respect. Money can be a delicate subject to say the least. Combine that with the fact that we all have our own way of approaching difficult subjects, and the mood is set for a tense and frustrating discussion. So be polite and respectful, and remember that your spouse's habits have probably formed over many years, so don't expect them to change overnight.

Let your spouse open up. Sometimes we can get so wrapped up in our own concerns that we forget that we're supposed to be having a *family discussion.* Remember to listen, and try paraphrasing what your spouse has said to make sure that you understand his or her perspective.

Frame it as a "we" issue. It's easier to handle a difficult situation when you're both on the same page. For example, if the family budget isn't being followed, ask your spouse for ideas on how to fix it together. Finger pointing is counterproductive, especially on a money date!

Write it down. At the end of your discussion, if an agreement has been reached or an important decision has been made, write it down. This isn't to be used to point fingers if mistakes are made in the future. Instead, it serves as a written reminder of the plan that you developed together.

Don't forget to celebrate. When you achieve a goal, no matter how small, celebrate it! It's easy to focus on defeat, but taking the time to acknowledge an achievement is even more important.

CHAPTER 2

Taking Your Financial Snapshot

In order to achieve the goals that you set in the opening chapter, you'll need to first determine your starting point. As you complete the following exercises, you'll have a much clearer picture of your financial status and you'll see what parts of your plan are in good working order, and what parts need to be improved. But keep in mind that even if you're nowhere near where you want to be today, I have good news for you: *This is just your starting point.*

If you begin feeling frustrated and maybe a little defeated, use that energy to push yourselves even harder towards achieving your goals. This chapter is not meant to highlight your weaknesses, but instead it's designed to help recognize where you are today, so you'll be able to track your progress from this point forward.

Find Your Net Worth

Think of your net worth as a financial snapshot. It captures where you are at a specific moment in time. It will change month to month, and should improve over time. So how do you calculate your net worth? At its heart, the simple formula is: Assets - Liabilities = Net Worth

What are your assets? They include the cash in your bank account, the investments in your retirement accounts, your car, your home, etc. Your assets are the things that you own.

Your liabilities are your debts like credit cards, auto loans, student loans, and your mortgage. Your liabilities are the things that you owe.

Depending on your present situation, some items like your house may fall into both categories. Your home's value is an asset, and your remaining mortgage balance is a liability.

To help you remember all of your assets and liabilities, the National Association of Personal Financial Advisors (NAPFA) provides the following list of documents that you should gather to assemble your net worth.

- Bank records
- Credit card statements
- Debt statements
- Investment account statements
- Retirement account statements
- Titles and deeds to properties

You can either manually list your assets and liabilities on a spreadsheet and tally them up, or if you prefer a more high-tech option, you can use web-based software like Personal Capital, Mint, You Need a Budget, or EveryDollar.

You'll need to spend anywhere from thirty minutes to an hour setting up your net worth snapshot, but moving forward it will be incredibly easy for you to track and update your net worth.

Tracking Your Income and Expenses

Now that you've reviewed your assets and liabilities and found your net worth, we're next going to focus on your cash flow. Specifically, we'll be looking at your income and expenses to see what patterns we can find.

First, login to your bank and credit card accounts and pull up last month's transactions. Then print out the transaction reports and mark each transaction as follows:

- If the expense is a necessity like rent or food, mark it with a #.
- If the expense helps you get closer to your goals outlined in Chapter One, mark it with a *.
- If the expense brings you true joy, mark it with a ^.
- Leave everything else blank.

At this stage, it's important not to nitpick over why your spouse may have spent money on a particular item, or why a certain spending category may be higher than you thought. That's not the goal. Instead, I want you to become aware of where your money is currently going by focusing on the symbols. If you're like me, you'll be amazed at how much spending you do unconsciously.

Now put a pin on what you've seen today, we'll come back to this later when we create a budget that you'll both love.

Why Tracking Your Money Matters

Consistently tracking your net worth and cash flow will help reduce tension during your money dates and it promotes open communication. When you have the numbers in front of you, it provides an objective focal point to talk about as a couple. Since money can be a delicate subject, sticking with the hard numbers allows you to attack the problem and not each other.

Knowing your key numbers also serves as a great motivator for change. You'll be able to clearly see, in black and white, how much money you're spending and how much debt you have. You'll discover ways to cut back each month until your numbers are more in line with your expectations.

Money Date #2: Create Your Vision Board

This date night is going to be a little more typical than your first money date. I suggest making this a relaxing night in, as you'll have some work to do.

Celebrate Your Wins

Start this date, as always, by celebrating your wins. It may seem small to you, but forming goals as a couple and dedicating yourselves to achieving them is a big achievement. And if you're a step or two closer to finding your "why," that's worth celebrating, too.

Review Your Goals

Reminding yourselves of your goals on a daily basis is the key to making them a reality. In order to do this, one thing that I've found very handy is creating a vision board. You might think that sounds basic or even elementary, but it's a powerful way to stay motivated.

To get started, clip out magazine pictures that capture what you're working towards. Also print images that inspire you and remind you of your "why." Or, if you're more tech based, create a collage using a tool like Photoshop, Canva, or GIMP. You can then save the collage as a background image on your computer or tablet. The purpose is to create something unique that serves as a daily reminder about what it is that you want to achieve.

(If you find yourselves embarrassed to have your vision board where house guests or friends might catch it, put it in your master bathroom or behind your bedroom door. But make sure it's somewhere that you and your spouse will see it every day.)

Review the Numbers

We're now going to review your net worth and cash flow numbers. Start by reviewing last month's expenses, keeping in mind this is not the time to get upset over money already spent. Instead, I want you to look over last month's transactions with your spouse and see if you can pick out three expenses to reduce.

Pick one expense that you both agree needs to be trimmed. Then each of you should pick out one additional expense that you can personally reduce or eliminate. Once you've made your decisions, make a note. We'll use this on the next money date.

Deal With Hiccups

Have you recently experienced something that negatively affected your goals, net worth, or cash flow? If so, how did you handle it? Would you do things differently if the same problem occurred again? Why or why not?

Plan for Next Month

Just like the end of your first money date, I'd like for you to look ahead to next month to see if you anticipate any large expenses. Specifically I'd like you to focus on any purchases that might affect your net worth. Do you anticipate buying any big-ticket items or increasing your spending? Estimate how this will impact your net worth, and begin getting more comfortable with the idea of tracking your net worth on a regular basis.

WEEK 2

Creating Your Spending Plan

CHAPTER 3

———◆———

Building a Budget You Both Will Love

Congratulations! You've made it through week one and you've accomplished a great deal already. In a matter of days you've already defined your goals and gotten a clear picture of your net worth and monthly cash flow. Now it's time to dive a little deeper into your income and expenses by creating a budget.

The idea of a budget is simple; it's telling your money where it needs to go. At its core, your budget should do the following:

• Make sure that your household essentials are covered.
• Bring you closer towards achieving your goals.
• Allow you to enjoy life, both today and tomorrow.

Budgets Are Not the Enemy!

Whether you use the term "spending plan," "conscience spending," or "budget," one thing seems clear—people don't like to use them. In fact, a recent survey conducted by Experian found that 42 percent of all Americans don't currently have a budget in place. The most common reasons given? Respondents said they were ineffective and unnecessary.

Considering that in the same survey, 46 percent of respondents admitted they were not saving as much as they hoped, and nearly 75 percent said they were behind in their retirement savings, it seems clear that not having a budget can be detrimental to your money and marriage.

So why are we so apprehensive about creating a budget? From my experience, the most common reasons are:

- Having no real plan or clear vision for what the budget is meant to achieve.
- Trying to be perfect.
- Overcomplicating the budgeting process.

I'm going to help you work through these problems and show you the core principles that every budget needs in order to succeed. Then I'll provide three different budgeting methods for you to consider. They can each be customized to fit your lifestyle.

Creating a Starter Budget

When my husband and I created our first budget and determined how much we could spend and where we could spend it, it felt too restrictive. However, as we began to see our debt decrease and our savings grow, while still being able to spend money going out with friends and family, I started seeing our budget as a way of giving us more freedom and options.

Continuing our trip planning analogy from Chapter One, think of your budget as your car and your money as the fuel. Since you've already decided on your final destination, now it's just a matter of getting there. You can drive a Hummer that's big and flashy and will eat up a lot of gas, or you can choose a hybrid that will not only get you to your destination faster, but will use less gas along the way.

Your budget isn't meant to restrict you and keep you from having fun, instead it's your ticket to freedom.

Stop Chasing Perfection

Look, I get it. You want to get out of debt as fast possible and your budget is supposed to help you get there... So you start reviewing the numbers with your significant other and one of you comes up with the genius idea, "Hey if we skip eating out completely, we'll shave nine months off our debt-free date!"

Now, considering that the two of you *love* going out to eat, how well do you think this new budgeting idea will go? In most cases, you won't make it through the first month.

Instead, it's better to keep fun and enjoyable activities in your budget. Want to cut back on eating out? Cool. Just trim back. You can always make further adjustments later if you find lower cost alternatives that allow you to still enjoy yourselves.

Don't Make It Complicated

While you want your budget to be thorough and account for all of your income and expenses, the reality is that most people don't want to track (and stress over) every penny. It can be very time consuming and tedious, and can quickly become overwhelming. To help streamline the budgeting process, consider using one of the following apps.

Personal Capital. I use Personal Capital and find it to be user-friendly and comprehensive. This program not only allows you to create a budget, but it will also calculate your net worth, manage your investment accounts, and plan for retirement. Everything in one spot…Boom!

Mint. Very visually appealing, Mint allows you to set-up text alerts to monitor your problem spots, and it allows you to create customizable financial goals based on the income and expense information that you provide.

ProActive Budget. This mobile app is a digitized envelope system that allows you to track your spending in real-time with your phone. If you're a constant traveler or frequently away from your computer, Proactive Budget is a smart solution.

EveryDollar. If you're familiar with Dave Ramsey's baby step program, this app will seamlessly walk you through the steps. They also claim that it takes less than ten minutes to set up your first budget—perfect if you're busy and on-the-go.

You Need a Budget (YNAB). This powerful tool will guide you through a four-step process to construct your first budget. After adding your income, YNAB will also suggest a few spending categories with corresponding dollar amounts to help you get started.

Tiller. If you're a fan of spreadsheets, Tiller is perfect for you. The program allows you to create a custom budget through the use of an automated spreadsheet. It is currently the only budgeting tool that provides a daily automated feed of your bank data directly into a Google Sheet.

Tips for Creating Your First Budget

Before I introduce the three different types of budgets for you to consider, I'd like to share some universal tips to keep in mind as you create your sustainable spending plan.

Every dollar must have a purpose. When you create your budget, make sure that every dollar is being allocated to its highest and best use. You should regularly reevaluate your budget and make sure that your money is serving a specific purpose and helping you get a step closer to achieving your long-term goals.

Make sure that fun is in your budget. Being a miser is not going to encourage you or your spouse to stay on track and follow a budget for very long. Remember to leave room in your budget for fun stuff, too!

Save for rainy days. Life happens—cars break down, appliances fail and bills can seemingly start piling up out of nowhere. Prepare for these unexpected costs by re-membering to assign a portion of your budget towards saving money in an emergency fund.

Three Starter Budgets to Build Wealth

I'm going to let you in on a secret. The perfect budget doesn't exist. It seems like every couple I interview has their own way of making their budget work. Some love to use pencil and paper or simple spreadsheets, while others prefer high-tech apps. Some budget their money down to the penny while others prefer to focus on broad spending categories instead.

The following pages highlight three different budget-ing styles for you to consider, each with their own benefits and limitations. I suggest sampling each one to see which works best for you, and then making adjustments as needed to make it your own. (On your third money date you'll be creating your budget together. Details are provided at the end of this chapter.)

Budget #1: The 50/20/30 Budget

A common hang-up that people have when it comes to budgeting is the fear that a budget means having to do a line-by-line review of all their expenses and income. If that's you, a proportional spending plan like the 50/20/30 budget may be the perfect solution.

Basically, with a 50/20/30 budget, your net income is divided into three buckets:

- 50% goes towards essentials like rent, food, and necessary bills.
- 20% goes towards financial goals like paying off debt and investing for retirement.
- 30% goes towards lifestyle choices such as vacations and gym memberships.

The benefit of the 50/20/30 budget is that it simplifies the budgeting process by using only three broad categories, and it also ensures that you're not forgetting to save for your long-term goals. If you're new to budgeting, this is an excellent option.

Budget #2: The Zero-Based Budget

The premise of the zero-based budget is that income minus expenses must equal zero. Therefore every dollar must be accounted for. For example, if you expect to earn $5,000 next month, then you must allocate your expenses (the amount that you will spend, save, gift, and invest) so they also equal $5,000. The benefit of the zero-based budget is that it requires you to constantly evaluate how you plan to spend your income, but this can also be a drawback if you have little time to devote to budgeting.

From my experience, the zero-based budget has a definite learning curve, and the first few months will be an adjustment period. I've yet to see a couple create the perfect budget on their first try, so keep this in mind and give yourself a little grace.

To test this method of budgeting, consider using the EveryDollar app created by Dave Ramsey's team. It allows you to easily tweak your budget and shore up any money leaks.

Budget #3: The Couple Money Budget

I created this third type of budget to provide a system that is flexible and can grow with you over time. It involves learning to live off only one income, and it allows you to quickly build your wealth.

When we were first married, my husband was working his first full-time job out of college and I was working at an internship. I had no idea how long my internship would last, so we decided that we would use his income to cover our basic living expenses, and my additional income would be used to save for our long-term goals like retirement.

It relieved a lot of stress because we knew there was a second source of income that we could tap into if we had an emergency expense. As a couple, learning to live off only one income gave us the opportunity to really build wealth together. It truly made the most of our two incomes.

I've interviewed dozens of couples who have retired early, and the one constant that I kept hearing was how they learned to pay for essential expenses with only one income. The second income was seen as a bonus, and used to pay down debt, accelerate retirement savings, and build an emergency fund.

The benefit of this type of budget, along with retiring sooner and accomplishing your goals more quickly, is that it financially prepares you for potential job loss or a downturn in the economy. If you're already living off only one income, you will have to make fewer sacrifices if you're faced with an unexpected expense.

Regardless of the budgeting method that you choose, don't underestimate the importance of saving even a small amount of money each month. As the following chart demonstrates, saving just a few extra dollars per week can lead to significant gains over the long run due to the effects of compound interest.

Long-Term Effects of Increased Savings				
Monthly Savings	Value in 5 Years	Value in 10 Years	Value in 20 Years	Value in 30 Years
$25	$1,835	$4,532	$14,317	$35,440
$50	$3,671	$9,064	$28,633	$70,881
$100	$7,341	$18,128	$57,266	$141,761
$150	$11,012	$27,193	$85,899	$212,642
$200	$14,683	$36,257	$114,532	$283,522

✓ *Assumes an 8% annual rate of return.*

Why You Need an Emergency Fund

An essential element of any budget is an emergency fund. As you continue to build wealth and work towards your long-term goals, you're sure to hit some bumps in the road. Consider what would happen if your basement floods and you face a large repair bill? Or what if something as simple as a flat tire occurred? Has your budget taken these unanticipated expenses into account? Whether you need to come up with $150 to replace your tire or $3,000 to repair your basement, if you don't already have the money set aside in an emergency fund, all of the progress you've been making could be put at risk. This is why it's so important to not skip out on savings!

There are plenty of American households who don't have any savings at all—common estimates puts the figure around 25 percent. If you find yourself in a situation where you currently have no savings, or very limited savings, this section will help you develop a plan to protect yourself when the unexpected occurs.

To illustrate the process of building an emergency fund, I'll be using a fictional couple, Rob and Elle, to lead us through an example. While they may not mirror your situation exactly, I hope their story will provide perspective and show you how easy it is to start building an emergency fund.

Our couple, Rob and Elle, are tired of having one hiccup after another set them back on their road to becoming debt free. Based on some recent car problems they've been having, they decide that they want to have at least $1,500 saved in their bank account to cover future repair costs.

They've been paying an extra $100 per month towards their credit cards, but that money will now be used to build their emergency fund, instead. At their current savings rate, it will take fifteen months to increase their emergency fund to the desired level. Looking at their timeline, they decide that's entirely too long and they begin to review their budget to see what expenses they can reduce. They find that if they both brown-bagged their lunch just twice a week, they would save $30 per week, or $120 per month. They also decide to cancel two magazine subscriptions, saving an additional $20 per month. Adding this extra $140 to their previous monthly total of $100, their new balance now stands at $240 per month. They've reduced the amount of time that it will take to establish their $1,500 emergency fund from fifteen months to just over six months. Not bad, but they can do better.

Rob decides to sell some of his old collectibles on eBay and Craigslist. He makes an even $250. Elle does some freelance work on the side that brings in an additional $250 per month.

Now they can have their emergency fund ready to go in just two and a half months. Much better!

Where to Keep Your Emergency Fund

Once you've built up your emergency fund, the next step is deciding where to keep it. You should base your decision on three factors: ease of access, safety, and growth potential.

Easy access in case of emergency. When your refrigerator stops running or your washing machine breaks, you need your money *now.* It does no good to have your money earning a high interest rate if you can't access it quickly and when you need it the most.

Safe place to store your money. Make sure that your emergency fund is being held in an account that is insured by the FDIC (for banks) or the NCUA (for credit unions).

Future growth potential. If you can earn a decent interest rate for your emergency fund while meeting the previous criteria, then go for it. For us, we chose a high interest rate savings account from a reputable online bank. It offers us the security and easy access that we needed along with a competitive interest rate.

If you prefer a brick and mortar option, try a local credit union or bank. They may offer attractive introductory interest rates along with the safety and access that you're looking for.

What Counts as an "Emergency"?

Your emergency fund is basically for...well, emergencies. This is worth mentioning because many people mistake their emergency fund for their regular checking or savings account. It is meant to cover *non-routine* expenses that are otherwise impossible to plan for. If you anticipate a large expense in the weeks or months ahead, incorporate it into your budget rather than relying on your emergency fund.

For example, assume that you expect your car will need some maintenance and repairs over the next few months, but you're unsure how much it will cost. Look back over the past year and see how much you spent on car maintenance in total. Then divide that number by twelve and include that figure in your budget. That way you will not be blindsided when you receive your bill. If the cost far exceeds the amount that you budgeted, then is the time to consider dipping into your emergency fund.

How to Avoid Fighting About Your Budget!

Money fights are rarely about money. But how we spend or save money is, to a degree, a reflection of what we value and prioritize, and that can easily lead to disagreements. If you find yourself on the verge of a money fight, try to dig deeper and understand the root cause of the problem. Does your spouse still view his or her income as "theirs" to some degree? How does your spouse feel about earning more or less than you? When spending money, is a need being fulfilled, or is money being spent due to stress or boredom? By talking through these issues, you'll be able to better understand the cause of the disagreement.

Once you've identified the problem, next focus on finding a compromise. Sometimes striking a compromise is easy, but as I'm sure you already know, sometimes it can be a real challenge. Try to keep the following principles in mind in order to create a win-win for you and your spouse.

Remember to listen. It's important that each of you feel like you're being heard. As you're presenting your cases, make sure that you're actively listening and not just thinking about your counterargument.

Keep an open mind. You may each feel certain that your perspective is the right one, but remember that having an open mind will allow you to find a solution that makes both of you happy.

Be prepared to sacrifice. While we might not always get exactly what we want in the moment, compromising allows us to get what we want in the long-term—a happy marriage.

Find common ground. When all else fails, start small and try to find some common ground. Start with what you agree on, no matter how trivial, and build from there. It will go a long way towards reducing the tension so you can move closer to finding a solution.

Money Date #3: Create Your Budget

This date night is all about budgeting for your future. You've already established your starting point, set your final destination, and defined your "why." Now it's just a matter of moving forward together; it's time to create a budget you'll love!

Celebrate Your Wins

When we looked at your net worth and spending last week, I asked you to write down three expenses that you could reduce (one joint expense and two individual expenses). Go ahead and pull out your notes, you'll be discussing them shortly. But first, I want you to celebrate how far you've come and your dedication to moving forward as a team.

Review Your Goals

Take a few minutes to review the vision board that you created last week. Now that you've learned more about the budgeting process and have a clearer understanding of how much you earn and how much you spend, does your vision board need to change? Have any of your original goals been updated? Are there any new goals that you'd like to add? Make the changes together, or write down your thoughts and update your board over the next few days.

Review the Numbers

It's time to put your money where your mouth is and actually create your budget. Regardless of the budgeting method that you choose, remember that the fundamental idea behind a budget is to make sure that your money is going towards what's important to you. It's about bringing you a step closer to your "why."

To help guide you as you create your first budget, let's assume that you'll be using an Excel spreadsheet on your computer. On the far left column of the spreadsheet (Column A), list your sources of income at the top and your financial obligations underneath. In Column B, list the projected dollar amounts attributed to each line item for the following month. Continue in Columns C, D, E, and so on until you've created a budget for the next twelve months.

Each month, when you sit down to review your budget, add a new column to the right so that you are always planning a full year ahead. Make sure that you're revising your numbers as needed.

Once you've made your first pass through assembling your budget, add up your expenses and deduct them from your income to determine your net financial status.

Review the sample provided on the following page to see how you might set up your spreadsheet. Remember this is only a guideline, and you should customize yours to fit your individual needs.

	A	B	C	D
1	**Income**	**Month 1**	**Month 2**	**Month 3**
2	Job 1			
3	Job 2			
4	Dividends			
5	Interest			
6	Pension			
7	Gifts			
8	Misc.			
9	**Total Income**			
10				
11	**Expenses**			
12	Housing			
13	Food			
14	Insurance			
15	Transportation			
16	Personal			
17	Utilities			
18	Gifts			
19	Health			
20	Savings			
21	Misc.			
22	**Total Expenses**			
23				
24	**Profit (Loss)**			

To demonstrate the budgeting process in greater detail, let's run through an example together. Assume that our sample couple, Rob and Elle, earn a net monthly income of $5,500 ($3,500 for Rob and $2,000 for Elle). They would like to use budget #3 (Couple Money budget) detailed earlier in the chapter. Here's how they might break down their budget.

Expense	Guideline	Amount
Housing	30%	$1,050
Food	15%	$525
Insurance	15%	$525
Transportation	10%	$350
Personal	10%	$350
Utilities	10%	$350
Gifts	5%	$175
Health	5%	$175
Savings	Elle's entire income	

The chart provides sample guidelines that you can follow, but it will be up to you to decide the exact dollar amounts to allocate in your budget. Keep in mind, the point of the Couple Money budget is that you're trying to live off *only one income.* That is why the entire second income is being applied towards the savings category.

Deal With Hiccups

Has anything occurred since your last money date that negatively affected your goals, net worth, or cash flow? If so, how did you handle it? Would you do things differently if the same problem occurred again? Why or why not?

Plan for Next Month

Are there any events occurring over the next month that might require you to dip into your emergency fund? If the answer is "yes," then go back and add that item to your budget before you forget! Your emergency fund is for *unforeseen expenses only*, so if you anticipate a large expense or two in the next few weeks, start planning for it now.

CHAPTER 4

———•———

Making Your Money Work for You

In this chapter, I'm going to help you create a financial system that meets your needs and simplifies your life. The words "financial system" sound intimidating, I know, but it simply means setting up your bank accounts so that your money is working for you, and not against you.

First, you'll need to decide if you're going all in with your spouse and using a joint account, or if you're going to keep accounts separate, instead.

Maintaining a joint account definitely has its advantages. Along with helping you work better as a team, it also benefits you in the following ways.

Less hassle with bills. By combining your money into one pot, you can simply schedule all of your bill payments from one central location. All you need to do is login to your account just to verify that all of your bills have been paid.

More transparency. Having a joint account is handy because it allows you to quickly identify where you can improve your finances. It also provides a safety net to protect you because two heads are better than one. With each of you monitoring the account you'll be able to catch any double charges or unexpected service fees that much easier.

Makes you face issues head on. When you share a bank account, it helps to bring big issues (money and otherwise) to the forefront of your marriage. I know that for some couples, that possibility alone will push them towards keeping separate accounts, but believe it or not, addressing your issues head on can be a wonderful opportunity for your marriage to grow.

Are Separate Accounts Hurting Your Marriage?

If there are so many positive aspects to having a joint account, does that mean separate accounts are toxic to your marriage? Should you close your separate checking and savings accounts and merge them into one? Not necessarily. The answer lies not in the accounts themselves, but in the context surrounding your decision. If you and your spouse are going to maintain separate accounts, be sure to clearly discuss why, so both of you feel comfortable with the decision.

In our household, my husband and I have separate checking accounts that we use for personal expenses like gifts, lunches out during the week, and small purchases here and there that make us happy. But with that said, we do have access to each other's accounts, and when we review our finances we are sure to have a clear picture of all our account totals. We don't want to have any secrets between us.

Finding the Right Bank Account

If you currently have checking accounts at separate banks and would like to consolidate, or if you're opening an account for the first time, make sure that your new bank account provides the following features.

No monthly maintenance fee. I understand that banks have the right to charge fees, but I expect something in return. With most banks, I've found that increased fees do not come with any extra services or benefits. So be sure to look for a checking account that does not charge a monthly maintenance fee.

No required minimum balance. Most checking accounts pay very little (or zero) interest to account holders. So why would you want to keep a larger balance in your checking account than is needed to cover your bills? If you're considering a checking account that has a required minimum balance, keep looking for a better option.

Free online bill pay service. This feature is a must. As you setup your financial system, you'll want to automate certain aspects like paying your bills to save time and provide convenience and control. (Automation will be discussed later in this chapter.)

Conveniently located ATMs. Whether you open an account at a bank or credit union, you need a way to access your money after normal banking hours. Having your bank's ATMs nearby is also important because it will allow you to avoid fees from out-of-network ATMs.

Earn interest (if possible). Finding a checking account that pays interest is a bonus, but it's not a deal breaker. Accounts that offer attractive interest rates usually require large minimum balances and charge a monthly fee. But if you can find a free checking account that offers a reasonable interest rate, take it!

FDIC insured. Make sure that your checking account is insured by the FDIC (for banks) or the NCUA (for credit unions).

Credit Unions: You're the Boss

Before we moved to North Carolina, I used to do my banking at a local credit union in Virginia and I loved it. I received great service and wasn't getting charged fees of any kind. As a member, I had access to the same services offered by banks—checking, savings, and money market accounts—and I could also apply for an auto loan and mortgage.

So how does a credit union differ from a bank? The main difference is how they're structured. Credit unions are not-for-profit cooperatives that serve their members. When you join a credit union, you are part owner. While a bank may reward shareholders, credit unions return their surplus income to their members in the form of dividends, better interest rates (for both deposits and loans), and other benefits like lower overdraft fees and lower fees for using an out-of-network ATM.

In addition to these benefits, surveys show that credit unions have higher customer satisfaction, too. My experience with credit unions has been positive, and the community feel and personal attention that I received appealed to me.

How to Join a Credit Union

While banks will allow just about anyone to open an account, credit unions require membership. Years ago, many credit unions were based around an employer such as a school system or state government. Today, there are credit unions based on numerous bonds such as geographic location, membership in a common organization, and affiliation with a particular church or school.

As you can see, membership opportunities have expanded to the point that there is probably a credit union that you will qualify for in your area. You may also apply to join a credit union if a close relative is already a member.

Putting Your System into Practice

Now that you've reviewed the merits of separate vs. joint accounts with your spouse, and you've found the perfect place to open your accounts, it's now time to put your financial system into practice. I'll guide you through each of the three budgets discussed in Chapter Three and show you how to implement them into your financial system.

50/20/30 Budget

Let's assume that you've chosen to use the 50/20/30 budget, and you're putting all of your income into your joint checking account, joint savings account, and retirement accounts. That covers the first 70% of your budget, but what about the remaining 30% that is attributed to fun money and lifestyle choices? I suggest using a joint account to cover these expenses at first—at least while you're still getting used to this budget.

The reason behind my suggestion is that it gets each of you used to the system and comfortable talking about money. You'll be making spending decisions that reflect your personalities, tastes, and values, and that provides a great opportunity to learn from each other and grow as a couple.

Zero-Based Budget

If you've chosen the zero-based budget, all of your money should be going into a joint checking account, where it will then be allocated to your expenses and re-tirement accounts. If you find that you're under budget, you should decide, as a couple, if you want to rollover the remaining balance to the following month or use it to pay off debt or increase your emergency fund.

Couple Money Budget

Finally, we have the Couple Money budget. Setting up your financial system with this type of spending plan is fairly straightforward. The income that is being used to cover your essential expenses should be deposited into a joint checking account. The second income should be di-vided into your savings account and retirement accounts.

How Automation Can Help

By now, you know that I believe the purpose of money is to serve as a tool to help you reach your personal goals. It's a means to an end, and nothing more. There's no rea-son that you should obsess (or stress) over it, when you don't need to. Setting up an automated system to help track your finances will go a long way towards providing peace of mind and alleviating a lot of unnecessary stress.

If you want to know why automating your finances is a practical move, consider my personal example.

There have been plenty of times when my husband and I have been swamped. Taking care of two little ones, giving attention to our marriage, as well as dealing with the demands of work has kept our hands full. But somehow we've managed to keep our budget and net worth from crashing and burning. The main reason is that our bill pay, retirement contributions, and other savings have become automated.

Without automation, we would have probably been late on a few bill payments and may have even forgotten to make our retirement plan contributions. By developing our financial system around the principle of automation, we're now able to check our account balances and make sure everything is running smoothly in five minutes or less per week.

Automate Paying Bills

Most banks and credit unions offer this time-saving feature, and in the digital age we live in, it's a must. It took me less than an hour to link most of our monthly bills to our checking account, including our utilities, insurance premiums, mortgage, car loan, etc. To do this, I logged into my checking account's bill pay feature and entered each payees name, address, due date, account number, and billing amount. The bank takes care of the rest.

Now that my automated system is in place, I only need about twenty minutes or so each month to review my bills and make sure that my payments have cleared. If I notice that a billing amount has changed from the previous month, I just login and change the amount.

Automate Your Savings

Next, automate the amount of money that will be allocated towards your savings account and retirement accounts. Refer to your budget to see how much you can afford to allocate to each of your accounts, and then talk to your HR department at work to set up direct deposits. Otherwise, set up recurring transfers from your checking account that coincides with your payday.

If your employer offers a 401(k) plan to employees, consider automating those contributions as well. Typically 401(k) contributions can only be made through salary deferrals, so be sure to talk to your HR department to enroll. Also find out if your employer offers a matching contribution. A company match is essentially free money, so be sure to contribute enough to your 401(k) to take full advantage of it.

Don't Go Overboard!

I love how automation has helped streamline my entire financial system, but it's possible to have too much of a good thing. With technology rapidly evolving, companies are regularly offering customers new ways to automate their finances. It can be tempting to sign up for multiple services, especially ones that offer to help you save time and money. But you have to remember that each time you sign up for a new automation service, you're giving up a certain amount of control and access to your money. You may one day discover that you've trusted your finances to a disreputable company if you're not careful.

To prevent this from happening, your best course of action is to thoroughly research any company or service that you're considering before handing over your sensitive information. Make sure that the company websites use multi-factor authentication and are secure. Review their Better Business Bureau ratings as well.

Remember, no one will care about your money as much as you do. Automating your financial system doesn't change that. Although it will significantly cut down on the amount of time that you spend paying bills and writing checks, you still need to remember to monitor your accounts regularly. Automation still requires a human touch.

Money Date #4: Create Your Financial System

By now you should be settling into a rhythm with your money dates. In fact, this will be the last of the "structured" money dates. For your upcoming dates, you can decide how often you'd like to meet and what details you'd like to cover. Unless you experience a major life event, your dates should be focused on maintaining the financial plan that you've already set up.

Celebrate Your Wins

Can you imagine how much easier your life will be once you've set up your financial system and automated your bills? You'll have fewer headaches, no more late fees, and more time to spend doing the things you love. Now *that* is worth celebrating!

Review Your Goals

Speaking of which, how are your goals coming along? Have you changed any of your long-term goals or the smaller milestones that you've set up to help you achieve

them? Have you had to make adjustments after taking another hard look at your budget? Or maybe you were playing it safe before and you've decided to up the ante. Have
you broadened your goals or found a way to achieve them
even faster?

Review the Numbers

Take a few minutes to review your net worth. If your
budget is sound and you're cash flow positive, then you
should be seeing your assets increase (through savings)
and your liabilities decrease (through debt payments). The
result should be that your net worth is steadily rising.
Even if the change is small, if your net worth is moving in
the right direction, go ahead and celebrate that win, too.

Next, focus on your budget. It's time to divvy up responsibilities. Review the different tasks involved and play
to each other's strengths. Remember, you're building a
system where you each contribute equally, and you're
both aware of your financial status at all times.

Who's better dealing with small details? That person
should set up the automated system and make sure all
payments have cleared. Who's great chatting it up? That
person should be in charge of calling your bill providers
and negotiating better rates.

You get the idea. The point is for each of you to take
the lead sometimes and to rely on your spouse at other
times. And don't worry, you can always switch responsibilities later if you need to.

Deal With Hiccups

I hope you haven't had any hiccups since your last
money date, but if you did, go ahead and talk about them

now. Was the problem something that you could have prepared for? Or was it a one-time incident that couldn't have been avoided?

Plan for Next Month

Discuss any special events or big decisions that you have coming up in the next month. Remember, it doesn't have to *always* be about money. These money dates are about strengthening your marriage as well as your finances.

WEEK 3

Boosting Your Bottom Line

CHAPTER 5

———•—•———

Save Money & Jumpstart
Your Finances

Week three is about boosting your bottom line. You'll learn how to save more money to jumpstart your finances, and I'll share some simple strategies that will help you accomplish your financial goals even faster. The truth is, you can save an incredible amount of money by making just a few small changes. You're skeptical, I'm sure, but I'm going to walk you through different money saving tips that will have a lasting impact on your budget.

Tip #1: Housing Is More Than Location

Location, location, location... This is the mantra of real estate agents, but it's not the whole story. When you're considering where to buy or rent a home, you need to go deeper and learn the neighborhoods. You *should not* be looking for swanky and popular, those neighborhoods are likely overpriced with minimal upside potential. What you want instead are the gems in the rough—the neighborhoods with the attributes you care about like safety, good shopping, quality schools, and well-maintained properties, but at an affordable price.

Also consider locations that are close to family or friends so that you can create your own neighborhood tribe. By trading skills and supplies with your neighbors, you'll be able to reduce your living expenses even more.

Tip #2: Avoid Auto Loans

After your home, your car is probably your next biggest expense. I remember when we were first married, I had a loan on my Jetta that turned out to be a huge weight on our already tight budget. We now avoid car loans altogether by buying our vehicles with cash. It might sound insane, but it's been wonderful. The trick is to do thorough research and find a car that will last for years with minimal maintenance required. Not having a car loan will free up your cash flow considerably. Not to mention, you won't have to worry about the added stress of an extra debt payment either.

Tip #3: Become a Frugal Foodie

Food is a big deal in my house. Not only because we love to eat (who doesn't), but also because, if you look at our budget, it's a major expense.

I'll preface this section by saying we're not big spenders—if the quality and taste are the same, the generic brands are our preference. Still, with a family of four, the cost of groceries can easily balloon and take up a large chunk of our budget if we're not careful.

To keep our expenses in check, we've decided to become frugal foodies. We use the following tools to help us get the most out of our monthly food budget.

Create a Price Book

In short, a price book tracks how much certain foods cost at different stores in your area. The goal is to help identify the best deals so that you will pay the lowest average price for your groceries. I know…it sounds old school and you're probably scared off already, but let me show you how it works and why it's so useful. Here are a few steps to get you started.

Make a list of items to track. Here's where people can overcomplicate the process. You don't have to track every little item that you've ever shopped for! Instead, look at your grocery list over the course of a few weeks. The chances are good that there are several staples on your list. Focus on those and ignore the rest for the time being.

Record as you shop. Visit your local grocery stores and record the prices and sizes for each of your core items. You can jot down the information in a notebook or use an app like Google Notes.

Review your results. Transfer the data onto a spreadsheet to quickly and easily figure out which stores have the best prices. Remember to compare unit prices to get a true apples to apples comparison.

Boom! You're done. You now can base your shopping trips on which stores offer the best value for certain products. You'll inevitably save money as the weeks go by and you'll learn ways to streamline the process as you get more comfortable.

Make Your Grocery Trips Go Further

If you want to shave even more money off your food budget, try these tips my family has been using for years.

Buy meat in bulk. We try to buy a good amount of our meat on sale, and then divide it up for several meals and freeze it. This tip saves time and money by reducing the cost per pound and requiring fewer trips to the grocery store. For example, when I get home from the store I'll break down ground beef into several bags for meatloaf, spaghetti, tacos, chili, etc.

Take advantage of sales (selectively). If you're like me, then you probably find yourself wanting to buy something because it's on sale, even if it's not something that you truly need. Sound familiar? When we do that, we're of course not actually saving money or improving our budget at all. If you catch yourself falling into this trap, make a mental note and walk away.

Don't forget coupons! Using your price book along with printable online coupons can be a powerful one-two punch that will drastically reduce your grocery bill.

Upgrade Your Cooking by Going International

One of my favorite ways to eat well on the cheap is by expanding my culinary skills. Don't worry, you don't need fancy cooking skills to pull this off. You just need to know how to prepare a few basic dishes that you can vary as needed.

It all starts with ingredients. What you have in your pantry will determine just how tasty your dishes will be. Fresh, high-quality herbs and seasonings can be an affordable way to expand your palette and sample some new flavors from around the world.

When I was researching recipe ideas, I went back to one of my favorite books, *The 4-Hour Chef,* by Tim Ferriss. In his book, Tim lays out regions of the world based on flavors in a cheat sheet format. While there were some unique items on the list, I was surprised by how many times garlic, onions, citrus, cilantro, and ginger kept appearing. It was the combination of these ingredients that creates unique cuisine. This means that with a few key ingredients, you too can create fun new dishes to try in your home.

Fortunately, these herbs and base ingredients are usually inexpensive and can be found in your neighborhood grocery store. But you can typically buy them even cheaper by shopping at an Asian, Latin, or international market.

Tip #4: Don't forget the Low-Hanging Fruit!

Every so often it's important to go through your budget line by line. I know that time is precious, but by carefully reviewing—and questioning—each of your expenses, you'll uncover multiple ways to improve your cash flow. Here are some of my favorite money-saving tips that you should look for when reviewing your budget.

Consider Cutting Your Cable Cord

If you're sick and tired of your expensive cable bill, here's a list of services to consider and negotiation tactics to try in order to save money.

Consider free TV with an antenna. Depending on where you live, you may be able to access free, basic television service using an antenna. One of the headaches, though, is getting a good signal. If you're unsure if using an antenna is a possible option for you, visit the website www.AntennaWeb.org, type in your address, and check your viewing options.

Check out satellite TV deals. The two leading satellite TV providers, DirecTV and Dish, frequently offer promotions and sign-on deals. In fact, it's hard to turn on the TV without seeing one of their commercials, and our mailbox seems to be flooded with their ads. Prices vary by location, but commonly advertised packages offer over one hundred channels for about thirty dollars per month. A two-year contract is typically required, and the promotional rate is only good for the first year. As always, don't forget to read the fine print!

Try streaming services. Even though we do not have cable, we still like to watch a few of our favorite shows and movies. We purchased a Roku streaming player last year (the Roku 3 to be exact), and we absolutely love it. It's an easy, inexpensive way to access multiple services like Netflix, Amazon Prime, Hulu, and more. In addition to these paid subscription services, Roku also offers some wonderful free channels, too. You can purchase a Roku at most discount retailers (including Amazon, eBay, and Wal-Mart) for less than a hundred dollars.

If you're interested in watching current TV shows, Hulu Plus may be the perfect solution. Members can access their content on a number of electronic devices such as their computer, iPod, Roku, or TV. Hulu Plus offers fewer ads for their shows, but unfortunately they're still included with a paid subscription. Like Amazon Prime and Netflix, Hulu offers some wonderful original content, too.

A third option to consider is Sling TV. It works by streaming your favorite television shows through the internet. They offer packages that include popular channels like ESPN, HGTV, and Disney. You can grab a subscription starting at twenty dollars per month, and best of all, there is no contract. Simply select a package based on the content you're interested in watching, and avoid shelling out your hard-earned money for channels you won't use.

Reevaluate Your Cell Phone Plan

I remember my first cell phone—it was a Nokia small enough to fit in the palm of my hand, and it had a screen that was so green I could hardly read it. That feels like a lifetime ago. Phones have certainly come a long way as they've become more central to our everyday lives, but cell phone bills have also steadily increased over time, too. If you're like me, tired of confusing contracts and pricey plans, consider using one of these alternative service providers.

Republic Wireless. If you follow my *Couple Money* blog, then you already know how much I love Republic Wireless. I first started using them several years ago when the service was in beta. What initially attracted me was their ridiculously low prices for unlimited talk, text, and data. Back then, they only offered one phone and one plan, but they have since branched out to offer multiple plans and phones to meet the demands of their customers. For more info, visit their site: www.RepublicWireless.com.

Ting. My closest friends use Ting and are extremely happy with their service. One factor that appealed to them was the ability to transfer their phones to Ting when they switched from their previous service provider. (Ting's website offers a compatibility checker so you can quickly determine if your phone can transfer.) Ting allows you to create a custom plan by choosing how much talk, text, and data you need. For most couples, this can be determined by checking your usage over the last year. With Ting, you'll be paying for what you will *actually use*, what a novel concept! For more info, visit their site: www.Ting.com.

Pre-Paid Discounters. If you want to keep your phone number and stay on a big network, a pre-paid service provider may be the way to go. A few of the most popular options to consider are Straight Talk, Boost Mobile, and Virgin Mobile. Each offer affordable plans and unlimited talk, text, and data options.

Tip #6: Become a Savvy Shopper

I'm all for saving money, but I don't consider myself cheap. When I was a college student, I would buy items solely based on price. Now though, I know better and I look for value. That means that I'd rather pay a little more to buy something of higher quality that will last longer.

Let's take furniture, for example. When you need a small table that's purely decorative, then it's fine to buy the one on sale at your local discount store. However, if you're looking for beds, bureaus, desks, and couches, then it will pay off in the long run to buy something of quality.

In this section, I'm going to show you how to become a savvy shopper and get the best value for your dollar.

Know Where to Shop

It had been years since I had last visited a thrift store. Shopping at these stores had been a regular habit during my college days, but since then I had developed the notion that it was impossible to find anything of quality in places like these. Sure, I might be able to find something that would do in a pinch, but nothing fantastic. Boy, was I wrong.

I recently rediscovered these unique stores and learned that it's possible to find treasures anywhere. It started when I visited a children's consignment shop around the corner from my house. The owners meticulously screened what they accepted, so the inventory was of fabulous quality. I was able to find new (yep, with tags still on) and gently used clothes and baby gear at ridiculously low prices. And it wasn't just clothes, but also cribs, toys, and even big-ticket items like furniture, too.

Most cities across the U.S. have plenty of similar stores, you just need to start looking. If you don't know of any thrift stores in your area, try searching your zip code at www.TheThriftShopper.com.

Bonus Tips For Buying Furniture

Before buying a particular piece of furniture, ask yourself the following questions.

Who will be using it (and where)? Sure, you want something that is great in form and function, but if you're looking at coffee tables, for example, remember that your children and their tiny friends will be around it constantly, so keep that in mind and narrow your search accordingly. It does no good to purchase a cute piece that you're constantly worrying about because of children or pets.

How frequently will it be used? When you're on a budget, consider spending extra for furniture that will get a lot of use, and spend less on background pieces that will receive less attention.

Does it fit with my style? Eclectic can be great, but if you think your potential purchase will clash with your other pieces, then it's okay to pass on it. There are plenty of other fish in the sea.

How is the quality and condition? Make sure that you get a thorough look at each piece of furniture before buying it. You should specifically look at the construction quality and the current condition.

As far as construction goes, you're looking for something solid that will hold up for many years. You'll save money over time by paying more upfront for a well-crafted piece instead of replacing it every few years.

When examining the condition, it's best to ignore any minor scuffs and blemishes. You can always re-stain or paint later. Today, you're making sure the item is usable and sturdy.

Do I have the DIY skills needed? Only buy a piece of furniture in need of some TLC if you have the DIY skills to bring it back to life. If you can't hang a shelf straight, you may want to skip the buffet that needs a lot of do-it-yourself love. But if you're handy and have the time and energy to refurbish an item, then go for it. Not only are you saving money, but you're also reusing and repurposing an old item which is great for the environment, too!

Tip #7: Embrace DIY

Although not everyone is equipped to bring an old piece of furniture back to its former glory, there are assuredly a few small projects around your house that you can tackle in your spare time. And not all DIY projects need to be dull and boring! I'll show you how to explore hobbies like homebrewing to both learn something new and save money at the same time. Here are a few of my favorite DIY projects for you to consider.

Repairing Electronics

Back in my high school and college days, I learned how to assemble a desktop computer and handle basic repairs not because I was particularly savvy with technology, but because I was flat broke. After I graduated from college and began working full time, I found myself too tired (a.k.a. lazy) to do those projects any longer. Basically, if it was more complicated then popping off the case and inserting a battery or chip, I passed on fixing it.

Recently though, I've began tackling projects around the house again, and I've gained some confidence as I've started to do more repairs and upgrades. While there are some devices that are pretty much designed *not* to be opened (I'm looking at you, iPod!), a good number of electronics can be easily fixed.

If you're on the fence about attempting to repair your own electronics, keep in mind that you don't have to jump into complicated repairs and upgrades right away. Just like with your finances, you can start small and move on to bigger projects as your confidence grows.

If you'd like to learn more but don't know where to start, I've got you covered! Here are a few of my favorite sites that can help you learn handy new repair skills.

iFixit. This fantastic site offers some of the best guides I've ever seen on how to repair popular devices, including Apple products. It's a community-based platform where users like you and me contribute repair tips that we've acquired over the years.

YouTube. This is usually my next stop after iFixit, and although the quality can vary, there seems to be a video tutorial for nearly every electronics problem known to man. Not too long ago I was able to find a helpful video on how to replace the broken lens on my old flip cam. Who knew!

WikiHow. You can sometimes get lucky and find a tutorial on how to fix your electronic device on WikiHow. Again, the quality varies, and for some repairs, pictures aren't enough. But still, it's a useful (and free) resource worth considering.

Google. When in doubt, Google it. But beware, some sites offer "free guides," but will then try to hard-sell you the required replacement parts. That is fine by me, provided the prices are competitive. So take your time and make sure that you're getting a good deal on parts before completing the purchase.

Homebrewing

Our motivation to try homebrewing was fueled by a fun tour of our local breweries here in Raleigh. After talking with friends and family who had homebrewed before, we decided to purchase a beginner's recipe kit and give it a try.

Assuming that you're new to the process of homebrewing, a recipe kit comes prepackaged with all the ingredients you'll need to make a batch of beer, including malt (perhaps in extract form), hops, and yeast. The exact amounts are included, so you can simply follow the recipe and enjoy.

....

Our local home brew shop sells recipe kits (as most do), but if you're buying online, I suggest trying Brooklyn Brew Shop. Visit their site at www.brooklynbrewshop.com to purchase a starter kit.

....

Since my husband and I sometimes have different tastes in beer, we wanted a set up that would allow us to brew two batches at a time. This turned out to be easier than we thought. The time added was minimal, and the extra cost basically amounted to grabbing an extra bucket.

As we became more comfortable with the process, we decided to experiment. We would swap out a few ingredients from different kits if we wanted our beer more or less malty, and we found recipes that worked for our individual tastes. (If you decide that you'd like to experiment with different recipes, an app like BeerSmith will come in handy. There you can share, view, and download different recipes from around the world.)

You may be wondering if homebrewing actually *saves* money, or if it's more a labor of love. The short answer is, it depends. Let me take you through our numbers.

Recipe Kit	Cost	Bottles*	Cost per Bottle
American Amber Ale	$33.50	50	$0.67
Dry Stout	$34.50	50	$0.69
Chocolate Maple Porter	$15.00	10	$1.50
Honey IPA	$15.00	9	$1.67

* Assumes 12 ounce bottles.

As you can see, the five gallon brews—which typically produce around fifty bottles—are very cost effective. In general, you'll find they are less expensive than what is sold in stores, and they taste a lot better too!

While I believe that you can save money by brewing your own beer, it really depends on factors like how often you drink, how much you drink, the type of beer that you prefer, and, of course, your schedule. But all of that aside, homebrewing can be a fun activity for you to enjoy as a couple!

Tip #8: Learn to Have Fun on the Cheap

When my husband and I first met, we were both in college, so our budgets were tight to say the least. But that didn't stop us from catching concerts, eating out at the local hot spots, and enjoying festivals and events. We found that with a little bit of planning, twenty dollars could actually go pretty far.

You too can make memorable dates together by giving it the old college try. Use these dating hacks to date like college kids and save on your budget.

Check out campus life. Speaking of college, why don't you check your local campus to see if there's any fun events coming up? Seeing campus productions of plays, attending sporting events, or going to concerts can be a great—and inexpensive—way to spend a Saturday evening.

Tour a brewery. Find a local brewery in your area and take a tour. Once you're finished, compare notes over a couple of pints.

Don't forget happy hour! One of our favorite spots for happy hour is a hole in the wall that offers fifty cent tacos and half-priced drinks. For the best deals, visit a happy hour near a college campus. Thirsty college students are big business, so the prices are sure to be competitive.

Enjoy a concert. Up and coming bands can offer a better bang for your buck; check them out at smaller local venues and college campuses for a more intimate and enjoyable experience.

Go on a lunch date. Between kids and work, sometimes it can hard to find time together in the evening. Lunch dates are a great solution. Have a picnic at your favorite park or grab something from a food truck, either way it's cheap but good eats.

Appreciate the architecture. When my husband and I went to Charleston for our anniversary, we spent a good deal of time just walking around and admiring the architecture. See what makes your city unique and take pictures of your favorite places and designs.

Visit town festivals. Find your community calendar and see what free festivals are going on this month. These are a great way to take in some culture and unwind with friends and family.

Tip #9: Think Twice Before Lending Money to Family

No, I don't think that your loved ones are intentionally trying to sabotage your marriage and finances when they ask you to lend them money, but those are the indirect consequences more often than not. If you follow my blog and podcast, then you know this is a popular subject that I like to cover. In fact, even years later, the number one downloaded episode of *The Couple Money Podcast* is about lending money to family! I could write an entire book on this topic, but instead let me lay down the most important points that I'd like you to consider before loaning money to family or friends.

Are You Helping or Hurting?

When you're approached for a loan by family or friends, be upfront and tell them that you need to run it by your spouse before making a decision. It's important to understand that as a married couple you *both* have a say in how your money is spent. Discuss the possible situations that might come up if you decide to make the loan. Trust me, a little preparation can go a long way.

No matter what, don't feel pressured into making an immediate decision. I know this can be difficult, especially if it's a close family member in an emergency situation, but you need to take the time to think the decision through. Let them know that you will get back to them as soon as you can, but you need some time to run the numbers first. Any reasonable person will understand, and those who love you will not want to cause additional stress to your family. If they balk and try to guilt you into making a snap decision, then you'll know what they're really interested in.

Let's say that you've run the numbers and decided that you *can* afford to help. Consider if making a loan is the best way to offer assistance, or if it will only provide a short-term solution to a long-term problem. If you think that lending money to your loved one will only make the situation worse, then consider the following suggestions.

Gift a small amount instead. Consider offering a small cash gift rather than a large loan. Make sure that the amount you're willing to give doesn't damage your budget. Your expectation should be that you'll never see the money again.

Address the problem directly. There are certain instances when lending money to a loved one will actually compound the problem by masking the real issue at hand. Offer to help by addressing the core problem that led to needing an emergency loan in the first place.

Offer to help with budgeting. Offer to share your personal budget and discuss what has worked for you and what hasn't. Don't forget to offer plenty of encouragement along the way.

Just say no. When all else fails, don't be afraid to politely say no. Sometimes tough love is the best option. Just make sure that you and your spouse are on the same page and comfortable with the decision.

CHAPTER 6

Side Hustle Nation

Spending less than we earn is a necessity for our financial plan, but we often focus only on the former and not the latter. As you continue to refine your financial system, you should apply as much effort to boosting your income as you do reducing your expenses. Here are a few of my favorite ways to increase income and quickly improve cash flow.

Find Your Side Hustle

We're living in a time when the opportunity to earn money and utilize our talents is plentiful. Just look at services like Airbnb and Uber that turn idle resources into cold hard cash. These opportunities to generate income, along with side jobs like running deliveries and doing freelance work, are collectively known as "side hustles."

For some, a side hustle serves as a way to pay off debt or save extra for retirement. For others, it's a way to explore a new career without going "all in" and quitting a full-time job. Either way, they're taking advantage of the abundant opportunities available today, and they're protecting themselves by diversifying their income.

While side income might not be able to replace lost wages from a full-time job, it can definitely soften the blow if you get laid off or your work situation becomes unbearable.

Look Before You Leap

Jumping in and trying a new side hustle can be tempting, but a word of caution: Choose your hustle carefully and treat it like a real business. Otherwise, you'll find that you're wasting your time and making little or no money.

In order to create a profitable side hustle, you need to consider both sides of the equation. You need to consider what you have to offer, and what your potential clients or customers need. Once you have defined each of these, you should be able to narrow down your options and identify the business venture that works best for you.

Let's start with you. Answer the following questions to help pinpoint your perfect side hustle.

- What are your skills, strengths, and interests?
- What are you good at? If you're a software developer, for example, what languages are you a master in?
- What are your best personality traits? Are you highly organized? Could you manage a remote team spread throughout the world?
- How do you spend your free time? Do you have a hobby that could translate into a money-making business?

Write down your answers and objectively review them. What are they trying to tell you?

Now let's move to the other side of the equation. Let's consider your potential clients or customers.

Besides being able to pay your fee (I know you were thinking it!), what do you know about them? What's their biggest headache? What causes them stress and frustration? Be as specific as possible.

Now look at all of your answers and write down the side hustle that fits your talents and serves the needs of your potential customers the best. Then tell your network of friends and family that you're open for business!

Become a Landlord

A side hustle that's growing in popularity is becoming a landlord. I know there may be some apprehension about renting out your spare bedroom to a complete stranger, and it's completely natural to feel that way. In fact, I've had some minor issues when I've rented out rooms in the past, but nothing has discouraged me from continuing so far.

I'm also not going to say that finding a reliable roommate is an easy task. It's important to remember that finding *the right roommate* is more important than finding *any roommate*. Don't let the thought of financial relief from the rental income cloud your better judgment and let just anyone move in.

Get It In Writing

Whether you rent to family, friends, or strangers, make sure that you have the agreement in writing.

There are contract templates that you can download online and tailor to fit your needs, but you should also consult an attorney to make sure that everything is on the up and up.

It's in your best interest to do your homework and make sure that all of your bases are covered, including background checks, tax planning, and complying with local regulations.

Declutter Your Home and Earn Cash!

One of my other favorite side hustles is turning unused possessions (i.e. junk) into cash. Start by looking around your house for items that you no longer want or use. Pay close attention to the following list which can readily be turned into extra cash.

Rarely used clothes. Most of us have too many clothes in our closet. Some articles aren't being used because they're in bad condition (throw those away), out of style (donate), or not our size (ding, ding, ding...sell these).

Collectibles. Some collectibles can fetch a decent amount of money, provided they've been kept in great condition. Scour your basement and attic for valuable collectibles that you may have forgotten about.

Musical instruments. If you're no longer using an instrument, let someone else experience the joy and make a few bucks while you're at it.

Once you've identified the items that you'd like to sell, check eBay and Craigslist to see if there is a market for similar items. If there is, you'll have a better idea of how fast they'll sell and what price you should sell them for.

Where to Sell

The most popular places to sell items are at a yard sale or pawn shop, on Craiglist, or on eBay. The key is to sell where you feel the most comfortable and where you can negotiate the best price. Some people prefer selling face-to-face, while others prefer the convenience of selling online. (A quick word of caution if you're selling online: Make sure that you don't get scammed! Never ship your product until you've received payment.)

As a final tip, don't be too attached to the items you're selling. Remember, you're selling them because you no longer use them. I've seen too many people let their emotional attachment lead to overvaluing their items and losing out on sales.

Negotiate a Pay Raise

This one's a bit of a curveball since it isn't a true side hustle, but it's a way to generate income and boost your bottom line nonetheless. You don't have to start your own business in order to get paid the amount that you deserve. Plenty of people are happy working for others, provided they are compensated properly. If you're an employee and feel that you're being underpaid, then learning the art of negotiating is essential. It will not only help you achieve a pay raise, but may also lead to other perks and benefits, too. In order to ask for a pay raise, I'd like you to consider the following points.

Be prepared. Before you approach your boss for a raise, make sure that you have a strong case prepared. Even if you know in your heart that you deserve the raise, your manager may be feeling pressure from his or her boss to push back. Prepare your talking points ahead of time.

Know the value of your skills. Do research to see what a competitive salary would be, based on your skills and experience. Dig deeper to see if you're fulfilling most or all of the responsibilities expected at that pay level. Knowing this information before approaching your boss will give you more confidence when negotiating.

Know your value to the company. It is your responsibility to make sure that your boss knows your accomplishments and what you contribute to the company. Keep a record of your achievements, including objective dollar values associated with them, and tactfully include them in your discussion.

Lead by example. Show what you're capable of by taking the lead on new projects in addition to your regular responsibilities.

Even if you don't get a raise, it doesn't mean that you should necessarily quit your job or start looking for a new opportunity. If your boss offered thoughtful feedback and constructive suggestions on how you could improve, then it was still a valuable exercise.

On the other hand, if you discovered that your company doesn't appreciate your efforts, or if your raise was turned down because the company is on shaky financial ground, then you should consider quietly starting your job hunt elsewhere.

CHAPTER 7

——•——

Effective & Efficient Investing

In order to achieve your goals, you'll need to develop an investment plan tailored to your specific needs. I know that may seem like an overwhelming task, but in this chapter I'll guide you through the process and show you how to create an investment portfolio in an hour or less.

The truth is, you can invest your money without having an advanced degree in finance. Despite what you may have heard, smart investing is not about picking stocks. In fact, unless you have extensive knowledge of the stock market and hours a day to devote to research, you should probably not be investing in individuals stocks at all. But before we get ahead of ourselves, let's start at the beginning. You first need to decide when you'd like to start investing, and how much you'd like to invest.

When Should You Start Investing?

One of the biggest mistakes that couples make is waiting until their next pay raise, or waiting until they're debt free before they start investing. (If we all waited for these things to occur, very few of us would ever be able to retire!) They feel like their small contributions today will have little or no impact over the long run, so they might as well wait a year or two (or more) to start investing.

What they don't understand is that they don't need a lot of money to start investing, and time is their biggest ally when it comes to growing their portfolio. In other words, there's no better time than the present to start investing.

Investing Now vs. Investing Later				
Year	Investor A's Contribution	Investor A's Account Value	Investor B's Contribution	Investor B's Account Value
1	$3,000	$3,240.00	$0	$0
2	$3,000	$6,739.20	$0	$0
3	$3,000	$10,518.34	$0	$0
4	$3,000	$14,599.80	$0	$0
5	$3,000	$19,007.79	$0	$0
6	$3,000	$23,768.41	$0	$0
7	$3,000	$28,909.88	$0	$0
8	$3,000	$34,462.67	$0	$0
9	$0	$37,219.69	$3,000	$3,240.00
10	$0	$40,197.26	$3,000	$6,739.20
11	$0	$43,413.04	$3,000	$10,518.34
12	$0	$46,886.09	$3,000	$14,599.80
13	$0	$50,636.97	$3,000	$19,007.79
14	$0	$54,687.93	$3,000	$23,768.41
15	$0	$59,062.97	$3,000	$28,909.88
16	$0	$63,788.00	$3,000	$34,462.67

✓ Assumes an 8% annual rate of return.

- Investor A contributed $24,000 total, beginning in year one, and A's account value is now $63,788.00.
- Investor B also contributed $24,000 total, beginning in year nine, but B's account value is now only $34,462.67.

Tools to Build Your Portfolio

The next decision that you need to make is which types of accounts you should deposit your money into so that you can begin investing. In this chapter I'll be reviewing three of the most popular account types: the traditional IRA, Roth IRA, and 401(k).

Traditional IRA vs. Roth IRA

An IRA is an individual retirement account. The biggest misconception about an IRA is that it's an investment, but instead an IRA is used to *buy* investments like mutual funds, bonds, CDs, etc. Although there are many different types of IRAs, the two most popular are the traditional IRA and the Roth IRA. The main difference between these two are the tax implications when you withdraw money during retirement.

Traditional IRA

If you or your spouse have earned income this year, then you're eligible to contribute to a traditional IRA. For 2017, the maximum contribution limit is $5,500 ($6,500 if you're age 50 or older) for each of you, or 100 percent of your earned income, whichever is less. (Refer to www.irs.gov for current year contribution limits.) You can open a traditional IRA at a brokerage house like TD Ameritrade, Charles Schwab, Fidelity, and Vanguard, and your contributions are generally tax-deductible. Once your contribution has been made, you're then able to invest your money as you choose with few exceptions. (Some of the exceptions that are not allowed in IRAs are investments in life insurance, precious metals, and collect-ibles like art and antiques.)

Once your money is invested, it will grow tax-free un-til you begin making withdrawals during retirement. Ex-cluding certain exceptions, you'll have to wait until age 59½ to withdrawal money from your IRA; otherwise you'll have to pay taxes and penalties.

Roth IRA

Unlike the traditional IRA, not everyone is eligible to make a Roth IRA contribution. You're only eligible to contribute to a Roth IRA if you're married and your com-bined AGI (adjusted gross income) is less than $196,000 in 2017. For single taxpayers, the AGI limit is reduced to $133,000. (Refer to www.irs.gov for the current year's AGI limits.)

The benefit of the Roth IRA is that your money grows tax-free, forever. Unlike the traditional IRA, you will not have to pay taxes when you begin making withdrawals during retirement. The downside? Unlike the traditional IRA, you don't get to deduct your contributions to a Roth IRA. Each year you'll need to decide between contributing to a traditional IRA or Roth IRA. Unfortunately, you can't contribute to both.

401(k)

A 401(k) is a popular savings plan offered by employ-ers that lets you, the employee, save money for retirement in a tax-advantaged way. Each year you can defer up to a certain amount of your income ($18,000 in 2017, or $24,000 if you're age 50 or older) into your 401k, which can then be invested as you choose. Similar to the traditional IRA, your money will grow tax-free until you begin making withdrawals during retirement.

In some 401(k) plans, employer's will agree to match a portion of their employees' contributions, and this is essentially free money. If your company offers a 401(k) match, you should at least contribute enough to take full advantage of the matched amount. If you don't know if your company offers a 401(k) plan or an employer match, be sure to ask!

Mutual Fund Review

After deciding which retirement accounts to contribute to, your next decision is what to specifically invest in. For first-time investors, mutual funds are a popular choice. Basically, a mutual fund is a collection of stocks, and a professional manager runs each fund. They are a convenient and affordable way to build a diversified portfolio.

"Loaded" vs. "Commission-Free" Mutual Funds

All mutual funds are either "loaded" or "commission-free." A loaded fund is basically a mutual fund with an extra sales charge. For example, a mutual fund with a front-end load charges a commission when you buy the fund, while a fund with a back-end load charges a commission when you sell it. A no-load fund (or commission-free fund), on the other hand, does not have a sales charge—although it will still have administrative costs that are represented as the fund's expense ratio. All things equal, it's best to buy no-load mutual funds and avoid the extra sales charge, but before buying any mutual fund you should first read the fund's prospectus. This is the mutual fund company's primary selling document and acts as the fund's owner's manual.

Beware of High Expense Ratios

The cost of running a mutual fund is passed on to investors by means of the expense ratio. This number represents the percent of a fund's assets that goes toward paying for the fund to be managed. A typical expense ratio for a mutual fund is about 2 percent, which means that an investor's total return will be reduced by that amount through the course of the year to pay management fees.

To avoid high expense ratios, many investors turn to index funds. With an index fund, you are simply buying an investment that tracks an underlying benchmark. For example, there are index funds that track the performance of the S&P 500, the international stock market, the bond market, etc. Since most of the buying and selling is automated and less active management is involved, the expense ratios are often less for index funds.

The next logical question you might be asking yourself is whether actively managed mutual funds (and their high expense ratios) typically outperform index funds (and their low expense ratios). The answer is a resounding "no." In fact, a study conducted by the S&P Dow Jones Indices found that over 85 percent of large-cap mutual fund managers failed to outperform the S&P 500 over the 10-year period through mid-2016. Mid-cap funds and small-cap funds also failed to outperform their indices by similar amounts, too (over 91 percent and 90 percent, respectively).

Target Date Funds

If you don't have the skills or knowledge to determine how your investments should be allocated between the different asset classes—cash, stocks, bonds, commodities, and real estate—then consider opting for a target date fund. These funds, also referred to as "lifecycle funds," are designed to make investing for retirement more convenient by automatically changing your asset allocation over time. They hold a mix of stocks, bonds, and other investments, and as you near retirement the mix gradually shifts according to the fund's investment strategy.

....

Even if you decide to invest in a target date fund, you still need to do your due diligence and research the fund on a continuous basis to make sure that it meets your needs and matches your tolerance for risk.

....

Common Investing Mistakes to Avoid

Even if you think you're more knowledgeable than the average investor, you're still more likely to benefit from following a systemic approach when it comes to investing, rather than going with your "instincts" and buying in to the latest stock tip.

It seems like every day we're bombarded with friends, coworkers, and experts declaring the best stocks to buy and sell. Fortunately, much of this is noise that can be ignored. Just remember to keep it simple, stick to the fundamentals, and try to avoid the following rookie mistakes.

Mistake #1: Trusting the wrong sources.

Choose your investment resources carefully and make sure they're credible. Ask yourself what their goal is and how they make money. And yes, that includes personal finance blogs, too. A good many, including my own, have partnerships with different companies to advertise their products. That doesn't necessarily make them less credible, but it might present a conflict of interest that you need to know about.

In general, any time you have an investment or tax-related question, you should visit www.sec.gov and www.irs.gov as your primary sources of information.

Mistake #2: Trying to time the market.

The next mistake that first-time investors make is not sticking to a schedule when it comes to making their retirement plan contributions. Instead, they try to time the market.

It's impossible to predict how the stock market will perform, so dollar cost averaging is the preferred method for making contributions. Dollar cost averaging means buying the same dollar amount of an investment each month, regardless of the share price. This means you'll buy more shares when the price is low and fewer shares when the price is high. It's a simple way to take the guesswork out of investing and avoid market timing.

Mistake #3: Not reviewing your portfolio.

The third mistake that investors make is failing to review their investments on a regular basis. Even when things seem to be going well and your investments are performing nicely, it's worthwhile to give your portfolio a checkup. Besides making sure that your asset allocation still fits your needs, you should also check to see if you're paying any unnecessary fees.

Is a Robo-Advisor Right for You?

Most couples that I meet are smart enough to manage their own investments, but they're also smart enough to know they don't want to! That's what the experts are for. But professional investment advice routinely comes with a high price tag that few can afford. That's why so-called "robo-advisors" like Betterment and Wealthfront were created. They're meant to serve as a practical solution for couples who want an uncomplicated, low cost, easy way to manage their investments.

At its core, robo-advisors offer investors portfolio management services by automating certain processes and eliminating the middle man (i.e. the investment advisor). This allows them to offer services for a lower cost than traditional human advisors.

In general, robo-advisors build an asset allocation model based on the investor's age, time horizon, and risk level. Having said that, not all robo-advisors are created equal. When choosing one to manage your money, you need to consider the following factors:

- Investment services: Does the company offer asset allocation, automatic rebalancing, and tax harvesting services? Are they comprehensive and thorough?
- Fees: While less fees are great, make sure the quality of service that you're receiving doesn't suffer because of it.

- Control: Do you want to allow the robo-advisor to make changes to your investments without consulting you? Are you willing to give up that level of control?
- Customer Service: Are you comfortable working with a completely automated service? Or would you prefer to discuss your investments with a traditional investment advisor instead?

CHAPTER 8

---·---

Protecting Your Family
With Insurance

When you think about setting up your financial system and building your financial plan, you need to look beyond investing and what's in your retirement accounts. Managing your money is a complete process, which means the stock market is just one piece of the puzzle. If your entire financial plan is based only on investing, there's no way you'll survive the next recession. It's during difficult times like these that a car accident, a house fire, or a medical emergency could devastate your plan if you're not careful. That's why you need to make sure that you have adequate insurance coverage that will protect you if an unexpected accident or loss occurs.

Understanding Insurance

I've yet to find anyone who gets excited about insurance (besides insurance salesmen). Best case scenario, you're paying for something that you'll never use. It sounds insane, I know, but that is the world of insurance.

The benefit of insurance, in my opinion, is the peace of mind that it provides. While we have little control over many things in life, we do have the ability to protect our family when the unexpected occurs. That's where the value of insurance comes in. When you have the right coverage for your circumstances, you're giving your family a safety net in case something unfortunate were to happen.

While there's insurance coverage available for practically every aspect of life, I'm going to focus on a few of the essential policies that you need to consider, namely life insurance, auto insurance, and homeowner's insurance.

....

Be sure to discuss all of your insurance needs with a licensed professional. Visit the National Association of Insurance Commissioners (NAIC) to find a referral in your state.

....

Life Insurance

It's not fun thinking about what will happen should you or your spouse die, but it's a necessity for your financial plan. Purchasing life insurance coverage when you're both in good health will make a potentially distressing situation a little less painful. You can also save on premiums the sooner you sign up for coverage. Each family's needs are different, but in general you'll need to purchase enough life insurance to cover the following items.

Time away from work. Losing a spouse is life altering and your family will need time to grieve. If you don't already have sufficient savings to cover time off from work, then you should factor that in to your life insurance needs.

Final expenses. According to the National Funeral Directors Association, the median cost of a funeral with viewing and burial is more than $7,000. Cremation is slightly cheaper, but still averages over $6,000 with the funeral included. Keep these costs in mind when deciding how much life insurance to purchase.

Financial assistance. Do you want to leave money for your spouse and/or children to cover debts and help with future expenses like college tuition? These expenses can add up quickly, so be sure to take them into account before buying coverage.

Auto Insurance

It's illegal to drive without auto coverage, so it should come as no surprise that selling auto insurance is big business. While it's always smart to compare rates between different insurance providers, you should also keep the following tips in mind to ensure you're getting the best possible deal.

Check your credit score. Did you know that your credit score can affect your auto insurance premiums? It's true, so review your credit report for errors and try to improve your credit score by making all of your monthly debt payments on time and in full.

Consider the age of your car. If you drive an older car with high miles, then it may not make financial sense to pay for comprehensive coverage. If you're unfamiliar with this type of coverage, it protects your car against damages that are not related to collision. Namely, it protects against fire, vandalism, and natural disasters. So ask yourself, if your car was to get vandalized, would you file a claim and pay the deductible? Or would you just purchase a new car?

If you would not file a claim, then you may not need to purchase comprehensive coverage.

Apply for discounts. Did you know that you may be eligible for a number of discounts that would reduce your premium? Don't be surprised if your insurance agent never mentioned these to you—you'll have to pick up the phone and ask for them, and you should! Auto insurance discounts are commonly issued for:

- Having an anti-theft device, air bags, daytime running lights, or anti-lock brakes
- Being claim free
- Having your car and home insured with the same company (the multi-line discount)
- Having multiple cars insured with the same company (the multi-car discount)
- Having a favorable vehicle injury rating
- Driving low miles per year
- Being a good student
- Being a long-term customer

Homeowner's Insurance

Homeowner's insurance is important if someone is injured on your property, a possession is lost or stolen, or fire occurs. When purchasing homeowner's insurance, be sure to keep the following tips in mind.

Insure the full replacement cost. When you meet with your insurance agent to purchase a policy, review your state property laws to ensure that your coverage is adequate and provides for the *full replacement cost* if your home is destroyed.

Talk to your neighbors. If you're curious about the types of claims that you might have to file, check with your neighbors who've recently had problems with their homes. If your homes were built around the same time, then yours will probably experience the same wear and tear, and by checking ahead of time, you'll be more prepared for potential problems to insure against.

Don't forget your possessions. Besides insuring your dwelling, your policy should also cover your possessions. To know how much coverage you need, take a thorough inventory of your personal property. Be sure to take photos and collect receipts for your items, so you'll be able to easily file a claim if an unfortunate event were to happen.

Apply for discounts. Just like with auto insurance, you may be eligible for homeowner's insurance discounts that you never knew about. Homeowner's insurance discounts are commonly issued for:

- Having a home security system
- Having your home and car insured with the same company (the multi-line discount)
- Being claim free
- Living in a new home
- Having smoke detectors
- Living within 1,000 feet of a fire hydrant
- Living close to a fire department
- Being a long-term customer

More Ways to Save on Insurance

Although insurance premiums can quickly add up and become a strain on your budget, fortunately there are money saving strategies that you can employ for each type of coverage if you know where to look and what questions to ask. Use these three tips to make sure you're not over-paying for coverage.

Shop around for the best deals. Insurance costs can vary widely from one provider to the next. That is why it's important to shop around and compare rates every year. You should either contact a few insurance companies yourself, or work with an agent who sells insurance through multiple providers. As you're reviewing quotes, make sure that you'll be receiving all policy discounts that you may be eligible for.

Bundle your policies. Purchasing multiple insurance policies from the same insurer can often lead to lower premiums through the "multi-line" discount. Nearly every insurance company offers this type of discount, and the national average is 10 percent.

Raise your deductible. The amount of risk that you're willing to assume has a direct impact on your insurance premium. That is why raising your deductibles will often lower your premiums. (As a refresher, your *deductible* is the amount of money that you have to pay out-of-pocket when you file a claim before the insurance company will make a payment. Your *premium* is the amount of money that you pay the insurer to keep your policy in force.) By increasing your deductibles to $500 or $1,000 for your home and auto coverage, you may be able to save a few hundred dollars each year in premiums.

Seek Out Specialists. Some insurance companies specialize in a particular type of coverage or demographic. For example, if you're a physician, dentist, or pharmacist, there are insurers who cater directly to your needs. Specialists can help insure against the unique challenges that are specific to your career. They can also better advise you on which policies you need to buy to protect yourself and your business. To find insurance specialists in your field, ask for a referral from the professional associations and organizations that you're affiliated with.

CHAPTER 9

How to Effectively Pay off Debt

To wrap up week three, we'll discuss how to boost your bottom line by paying off your debt. Even though most of us have strong feelings about debt, we often struggle to pay it off. We don't know which debts we should tackle first, and we don't understand how carrying large amounts of debt affects our ability to achieve our goals and build wealth. In this chapter we'll explore these questions together and I'll help you create a plan to become debt free.

When it comes to paying off debt, big wins are important, and it's what keeps us motivated to ditch our debt even faster. How relieved do you feel when you finally pay off a loan? Just imagine how amazing you would feel if you were completely debt free. If your hard-earned money was going towards growing your savings and achieving your dreams, how would you feel?

There are a number of ways that you can pay off your debt, and I'll be walking you through two of the most popular techniques in this chapter—the debt snowball and debt avalanche methods. Both methods are designed to keep you motivated and fully engaged in the debt payoff process, and they'll help you shave months off your debt repayment plan. Not only that, but they'll put you in a position where you can achieve your financial goals ahead of schedule, too.

The Debt Snowball

Financial guru Dave Ramsey is most associated with the debt snowball method. He uses it as a part of his system to help people gain financial peace. Paying off debts is the second of his seven baby steps, as popularized in his book, *The Total Money Makeover.* Thousands of people swear by Ramsey's method and have used it to pay off huge amounts of debt in a year or two. Here's how the debt snowball works:

- List all of your debts, excluding your mortgage, and arrange them from the smallest balance to the largest.
- Make the minimum required payment on each debt.
- Review your budget to determine how much extra cash you can put towards paying off your debts ahead of schedule. Use that entire amount to pay down the debt with the smallest balance.
- When the debt with the smallest balance has paid off, rollover the monthly payment amount to your next smallest debt.
- Repeat this process until all of your debts are gone!

The appeal of this method is that it's easy to follow. After all, you only have to focus on paying off one debt at a time. With the intense focus, it's supposed to motivate you to pay off your debt even faster.

Debt Snowball Example					
Debt Description	Current Balance	Term Remaining	Interest Rate	Monthly Payment	Payoff Rank
Visa card	$1,477	-	17.99%	$425	1
Boat loan	$3,982	17 months	3.00%	$175	2
Student loan	$8,735	31 months	6.80%	$224	3
MasterCard	$12,663	-	14.25%	$680	4
Car loan	$13,109	25 months	4.70%	$336	5
Equity line	$34,372	-	3.85%	$375	6
Mortgage	$168,487	240 months	5.50%	$1,510	7

There are modifications to this plan, such as using debt snowflakes to build your snowball, but the premise remains the same—chip away at the smallest balance first and then continue to the next smallest, and so on.

You may be wondering why interest rates aren't mentioned in this plan. The reason is that the debt snowball is about changing behaviors and not so much about getting the most financially pressing debt out of the way first.

While I know this plan is not for everybody, I do believe that many couples can benefit by using it. When you see your debts getting knocked out one after another, you're motivated to stick with your plan, and that's the real advantage—sustainability.

The Debt Avalanche

On the other side of the spectrum are those who hate paying a penny more to their lenders than is absolutely necessary. If this sounds like you then consider using the debt avalanche method, which involves tackling your debt based on the interest rate, rather than the balance.

The reason behind this strategy is simple: If you're truly committed to being debt free, then paying off your loan that carries the highest interest rate will get you there faster.

This method is just as direct as the debt snowball, but instead of applying extra cash towards the debt with the smallest balance, you're instead applying it towards the debt with the highest interest rate. Once that debt has been eliminated, move on to the debt with the next highest interest rate, and so on.

Debt Avalanche Example					
Debt Description	Current Balance	Term Remaining	Interest Rate	Monthly Payment	Payoff Rank
Visa card	$1,477	-	17.99%	$425	1
MasterCard	$12,663	-	14.25%	$680	2
Student loan	$8,735	31 months	6.80%	$224	3
Mortgage	$168,487	240 months	5.50%	$1,510	4
Car loan	$13,109	25 months	4.70%	$336	5
Equity line	$34,372	-	3.85%	$375	6
Boat loan	$3,982	17 months	3.00%	$175	7

Choosing the Right Method for You

While each payoff method is similar at first glance—you're tackling your debts one by one and building momentum as you plow through them—there is a different rationale behind each of them, and understanding that difference will determine your success or failure.

With the debt avalanche, you're interested in paying off your debt as fast as possible. You're motivated by the numbers and are determined to make sure that your lenders don't receive a penny more in interest than is necessary.

The debt snowball, on the other hand, focuses on the behavioral aspect of personal finance and assumes that small, quick wins will help you build momentum to tackle your next debt. You're more concerned with crossing the finish line rather than the speed in which you get there.

Regardless of the method you choose, be sure to automate your debt payments like we discussed in the previous chapter. And remember to schedule your payments early enough so you don't get hit with late fees!

Pay Off Your Debt Faster Using Snowflakes

After the initial thrill of starting your debt snowball or avalanche wears off, you might find yourself reaching a plateau. It's to be expected, considering there are only so many dollars that can be allocated toward debt repayment. So how do you fight through a slump and pump up your plan again? Welcome to the solution known debt snowflakes.

What are Debt Snowflakes?

Debt snowflakes are small, frequent amounts of money that can be used to whittle down your debt. These snowflakes are used to grow your debt snowball so that you can become debt free quicker. The key to using debt snowflakes is to remember that you aren't trying to go for big wins. Instead, the focus is on easy, small wins, where even an extra five or ten dollars can be applied towards paying off your debt.

Debt snowflakes have the power to speed up your debt snowball or avalanche not because of their size, but because of what they represent—the ability to adjust your money habits in small yet meaningful ways.

Consider Debt Consolidation

At the heart of it, debt consolidation combines your high interest debts into a single loan with a lower interest rate. A number of companies offer programs to help you consolidate your debt, settle with your creditors, and negotiate lower interest rates on your remaining loans. The monthly payment that you make on your consolidated loan includes a fee to handle these items for you. Think of it as a third-party payment system.

....

Be aware that fees charged by debt consolidators can vary widely, so be sure to shop around and read the fine print before signing up.

....

Depending on certain factors like your loan-to-value ratio and your credit score, you may be able to negotiate a better interest rate yourself, so don't be so quick to give up control to a debt consolidator unless you know the company can provide a service that you cannot perform personally.

If you feel like debt consolidation could be a good option for you, follow these guidelines to protect yourself:

Beware of aggressive counselors. When using a debt consolidator, you're giving up a certain amount of control over your finances. So think long and hard before signing up. If the counselors keep pushing you to make an immediate decision, or if they appear offended that you want to shop around, drop them.

Check their credentials. You can weed out possible scammers and fraudsters by making sure the company is registered with the Association of Independent Consumer Credit Counseling Agencies or the National Foundation for Credit Counseling.

Obtain a written copy. When you're interviewing potential debt consolidators, have them send over their terms in writing. Don't go by promises made over the phone. Make sure that you understand all terms and conditions, and also run the numbers yourself to make sure they check out.

Whether or not you decide to work with a debt consolidation company, you will still need to fix the root cause of the problem and not just treat the symptom. Changing your underlying financial habits is the only way that you'll successfully manage your debt.

WEEK 4

Choose Your Own Adventure

CHAPTER 10

How to Travel for Less

Congratulations on making it to week four! In this final week, our focus will turn towards using your wealth to live the life you've always wanted. Whether you choose to travel more, start a family, buy a home, or even retire early, I'll show you how to prepare your budget and avoid common pitfalls so you can enjoy your life to the fullest. We'll start this section by discussing one of my personal favorites—traveling, and the popular new trend known as "travel hacking."

I first heard about travel hacking from friends who traveled often for work. They would routinely accumulate points from their favorite airlines and use them to gain free flights and other travel perks. But it wasn't until I read Chris Guillbeau's book *The Art of Non-Conformity* that I saw travel hacking as a way to save significant amounts of money and have a lasting impact on my financial plan.

Chris was someone who mastered the system and used it extensively to travel the world for little or no cost. Sounds too good to be true, right? Actually it's not, but that doesn't mean it's for everyone. Read the benefits and traps of travel hacking later in this section and discuss with your spouse if it's something you should try as a couple.

But first, how exactly does travel hacking work? Essentially, you sign up for a credit card and receive an initial bonus along with a limited time offer for extra rewards. The bonus and rewards come in the form of "points" that you can apply towards travel discounts for flights, lodging, and transportation.

Why are banks, credit card companies, and travel companies so generous with these bonuses? Simple—it's because they expect their short-term losses to yield long-term gains if you become a customer for life. It's purely a numbers game. Keep this in mind if you decide to experiment with travel hacking. Make sure that you're aware of the terms and conditions that will apply after the promotional period has ended.

Should You Give Travel Hacking a Try?

Is the hacking system right for everybody? Absolutely not! But if you're disciplined and willing to follow a careful, systematic plan, then it can pay off huge in the form of deeply discounted travel.

Before diving into the details, you first need to decide if you qualify. If you currently have credit card debt, then *I do not recommend* trying this strategy. You'll only be hurting yourself in the long run and further damaging your credit score. But assuming that you pay your monthly credit card balance in full and have a favorable credit score, then the next question that you need to ask yourself is whether you have the self-discipline and organization skills needed to make travel hacking work. If these aren't your strongest skills, then skip to the next section.

Maximize Travel Hacking with a Community

If you want to experiment with travel hacking, I suggest joining a network of experienced hackers. There you'll find a number of best practices to follow and pitfalls to avoid. Some of the most popular and thorough groups include the following.

Travel Hacking Cartel. The cartel explains exactly what you need to do to accumulate frequent flier miles, and they also show you how to redeem your points to maximize your travel benefits. Their community will teach you about glitch fares, how to pad your mileage account, and how to earn elite status.

Upgrade Your Bucket List. This program will help you master the "secret codes" to use when booking hotels that will immediately drop the price, and they also show you how to gain access to the finest international airline lounges without paying high membership fees. Their focus is more on exotic and luxurious travel, but they also provide a great beginner's guide to domestic travel hacking, too.

Frequent Flier Master. Their featured motto is "free travel anywhere," and they offer the "one free plane ticket" guarantee. They will show you how to earn up to 200,000 frequent flier miles a year *without flying*, and how to bypass outsourced (and often unhelpful) airline customer support.

If you're instead looking to simply get better deals on travel bidding, then I recommend trying these fantastic resources: Better Bidding, Rate Drop, and Hotel Deals Revealed.

Debt-Free Vacations

My husband and I have always preferred to take debt-free vacations. They reduce stress, keep our budget in check, and don't interfere with our long-term goals. So what's the key to debt-free travel? Lots of planning and discussion. While it's possible to find some fantastic last minute deals, they're usually hard to come by. The more you delay planning your trip, the more likely it is that you'll go over budget and make up the shortfall with debt.

Did I just say budget? Yes—you should have a budget for your vacation, and your budget should include more than just your airfare. Remember to include *all* of your vacation expenses including lodging, transportation, food (overestimate with this), local activities, and emergencies.

As part of our vacation routine, we start by checking the basic travel websites. These are the sites you're probably familiar with, like Priceline, Kayak, Hopper, etc. We often find that it's best to split our trip between two sites. For example, we may book our rooms from Hotels.com and our airfare from Priceline.

Next, we need to decide if we're going to purchase travel insurance. This age-old question has no clear answer. You need to make the decision based on individual factors like your tolerance for risk, the airline/hotel cancellation policy, and the geographic region where you'll be traveling from. (Is there a chance that a major winter storm will decide to make an appearance the morning of your flight? If so, travel insurance may be a smart decision!) You should also check with your credit card company to see what protections (if any) they offer their cardholders in the event of a cancellation.

Vacation For Less

Once you've arrived at your destination and you're having a great time, don't forget to mind your money! If you're not careful, the spending decisions that you make when you're stress-free in the Caribbean might come back to haunt you when you receive your next credit card bill. Here are a few of my favorite ways that you can save money and still have a fabulous trip.

Eat Well. For us, eating out is typical when we're on vacation. We love trying different places and discovering new dishes. But rather than visiting the most trendy, expensive restaurants, we instead explore the town and ask locals for their homegrown recommendations. More often than not we'll find a hole in the wall that is adored by the community, and is both delicious and affordable. And after our meal we always remember to save our doggie bags to enjoy the next day at the hotel!

Save on Souvenirs. Depending on where you're vacationing, you may discover that chain retailers offer cheaper (and higher quality) souvenirs than the usual tourist spots.

While we were in Orlando checking out the parks, I noticed some wonderful gifts at the local Wal-Mart. We purchased the bulk of our souvenirs there, and only bought one-of-a-kind items at the actual park. That allowed us to not only save a lot of money, but to include more people on our gift list, too.

CHAPTER 11

——•——

Money Moves for Starting a Family

Becoming parents has made our lives so much richer than we ever imagined. Every day we're grateful and happy to have this opportunity. As awesome as it is, being parents comes with incredible responsibilities. When we first found out that we were going to have a baby, we knew that we wanted to take care of our finances quickly so that we could devote more time and attention to our newest addition.

There are many numbers commonly tossed around about how expensive it is to have (and raise) a child. During my pregnancy, I started keeping track of how much we spent preparing for our baby, and it was a real eye-opening experience. In this section, I'm going to share our costs with you, and also run through the expenses we incur today taking care of our two little ones.

What Expenses Can You Expect?

Every family is different, but here are some estimates for what it will cost to have a child. Although this information is only based on our personal experience and those of our friends, it will give you a good idea of what you can expect.

Hospital Bill

While we were pregnant I asked friends, both with insurance and without, how much they were billed for their hospital stay. For those without insurance, the bill was about $10,000 to $12,000 on average. For those with insurance, it was typically a few thousand dollars.

In our case, we received a bill from the hospital and our OB/GYN's office for $2,500. Our insurance had an above-average deductible, but we were fortunate that my husband's job reimbursed most of our expenses, and we were able to get a healthy discount by paying our remaining bills promptly.

Diapers

Babies go through more diapers than you'd expect. Even if you receive diapers as gifts (wonderful idea—put that at the top of your baby registry), you'll still need quite a few. The Bump estimates that newborn babies use an average of 75 diapers per week and up to 320 diapers per month. At about 25¢ per diaper, that adds up to about $1,000 per year! Tack on two boxes of wipes per month ($3 each), and baby soap, lotion, powder, oil, and diaper rash ointment (about $14 per month) and you have an additional cost of $240 per year.

Cloth diapers will save you money—if you plan to launder them yourself—but using a diaper service will cost about the same as disposable diapers.

Right now, we're using disposable diapers with our daughter, and to save on the cost we've joined Amazon Mom. With the diaper subscription service, we're saving 30 percent! For us, that means 190 diapers costs about $20 each month.

If you'd like to try cloth diapers, several brands have received wonderful reviews, including gDiapers, bumGenius, FuzziBunz, and Rumparooz.

Food

Whether you breastfeed or formula feed, please make sure that you're taking care of yourself and eating well. Having a baby keeps you on your toes, and you'll need to be as healthy as you can to keep up with your little one.

BabyCenter estimates that formula will cost about $105 per month on average. Adding solid food for your baby later on will add just a bit more to your monthly grocery bill.

Baby Gear

Babies are wonderful—and it doesn't take much to keep them safe and happy. If you haven't received certain items from your registry, hold off buying them until you need to. You may find you that don't have to buy nearly as much baby gear as you thought.

For example, some babies love bouncers and others can't stand them. My daughter received a beautiful baby swing from a friend whose son didn't like it at all. It was practically new and my daughter absolutely loved it!

Childcare

The cost of childcare varies greatly depending on the type of care (nanny, daycare, etc.) and the area you live in. According to the National Association of Child Care Resources, the average cost of center-based daycare for babies and toddlers is $972 per month, while the average cost for home daycare is $646 per month. Nannies are even more pricey, averaging about $2,400 per month for full-time care. I suggest using the childcare calculator provided on BabyCenter's website for more accurate estimates based on your individual needs.

Decorating Your Nursery on a Budget

When we prepared to have our first child, I remember my obsession with trying to make sure that our nursery was perfect. (I have since gladly embraced the concept of "good enough.") As parents, we want to make sure that our children have a safe and nurturing space. Yes, that sometimes means getting new pieces of furniture and baby gear, but it doesn't mean that you have to go broke!

Here are estimates for the average cost of furnishings found in most nurseries:

- Crib: $135 – $935
- Changing table: $90 – $275
- Rocker: $210 – $660
- Bassinet: $55 – $285
- Hamper: $25 – $65
- Mobile: $25 – $60
- Dresser: $90 – $550
- Baby monitor: $45 – $65

You probably notice that the price range for even essential items is huge! Depending on the brands that you buy, furnishing your nursery can quickly eat up your family budget. Fortunately, there are a number of affordable alternatives that you can use to find stylish nursery supplies for cheap.

Safety First

Let's not get carried away... Remember that safety is key when purchasing items for your nursery. You should always be willing to spend a little more if there's a safer alternative for your baby. For example, we bought our car seat new to make sure it had not been compromised before in an accident.

However, you shouldn't feel pressure to buy all new items. That's impractical and downright expensive. Your focus should be on purchasing high-quality products at a reasonable price.

Hand-Me-Downs

From my experience, family and friends are often more than happy to share baby clothes and toys that their children have outgrown. With a little luck, your nursery will have a full closet of clothes in no time. Just remember to pay it forward and show the same generosity when the time comes!

Yard Sales

Yard sales are always hit or miss, but if you're patient and willing to haggle, you might be able to walk away with some great treasures for your nursery. Remember these tips the next time you want to rummage through a yard sale.

Have your shopping list handy. Don't get distracted! Stay focused on what you need for your baby's nursery. It will help you save money and avoid cluttering your home.

Shop early. When it comes to yard sales, the early bird gets the worm. By showing up early and beating the crowd, you'll get first crack at the best items for your nursery.

Ask for a bundle discount. If you're buying more than one item, see if you can get a "bundle discount." It never hurts to ask, and you may end up walking away with the items you need in fewer trips.

Check the condition. It's not worth saving a few bucks if the quality is shoddy. Look for like-new condition (or better) on all items that you're purchasing for your baby's nursery.

Bring cash. Don't make the seller hold items until you return later in the day to pay for them. Have plenty of cash on hand and be ready to tote your stuff away after completing your purchase.

Craigslist

There are plenty of parents willing to part with their baby gear at very good prices on Craigslist. For sellers, it's a convenient way to get quick cash without the hassle of holding a yard sale. For buyers, it can be like shopping at a deeply discounted version of Amazon or eBay. But you need to be picky and carefully review the quality of the products. And remember to always assume that all sales are final!

15 Ways to Save on Baby Expenses

I asked some fellow parents for their best money-saving tips on how to save on baby expenses. While you may have tried a few of these before, hopefully they will inspire you to cut costs and regain control of your budget.

1. *Have a trusted friend or family member babysit for you.* If a loved one is babysitting for you, you're likely to get a great discount and you'll have peace of mind over your little one's well-being. But remember not to take advantage of their generosity! You should still compensate them for their services.

2. *Make your own baby food.* If you have the right kitchen tools and the time, go ahead and make your baby's food. It will not only save you money, but it will also allow you to introduce a variety of different foods to your baby early on.

3. *Buy baby supplies in bulk (when appropriate).* You can save quite a bit of money buying certain items in bulk, like diapers and wipes. Consider subscription services like Amazon Mom to save 30 percent on diaper orders.

4. *Shop consignment stores.* We have quite a few high-quality consignment stores here in Raleigh, and the same can be said for many places throughout the U.S. In fact, one consignment store nearby specializes in baby clothes and gear, and we picked up a few outfits between $1 and $4 each, with some having the tags still on!

5. *Cook at home.* Not exciting, but a huge cost saver. Eating at home not only helps you keep more money in your wallet, but you'll have more control over what you're eating, too. That means better health and more

wealth. Curious about what dishes to try or what cooking tips can save you time? Check out my blog *Married Food* for ideas.

6. *Watch your toy budget.* Babies don't need as many toys as you think. I know that it's tempting to get the latest and greatest educational toys that come out, but a few basic ones will go a long way. Plus, fewer toys have the added bonus of encouraging imagination.

7. *Buy for the long term.* Focus on buying baby furniture that is durable and will last for the long term. For example, when looking at cribs, be sure to check the material and design. You don't want the bed to break down after a move or two.

8. *Go generic.* Your baby can't tell if she's wearing name brand shoes or having her bottom cleaned by the store brand wipes. Save yourself some money and go generic!

9. *Buy washable nursing pads.* You'll go through these quickly, so I recommend investing in a few washable ones.

10. *Check out the clearance rack.* You can pick up some nice clothes and baby gear by looking at the clearance rack, but be sure to check for imperfections in the material and design.

11. *Keep the change.* At the end of each day, collect all of the loose change in your pocket, on the kitchen counter, and in your car. Trust me, it will add up quickly. You can use the money to save for your baby's future expenses, like a college fund.

12. *Take advantage of coupons and discounts.* Visit your favorite retail websites and search for coupons and discount codes to score deals on necessary baby items.

13. *Try free family programs at the library.* When your budget's in a pinch, remember that public libraries can be a great source of (free) fun and relaxation.
14. *Wait for the baby shower.* If you're watching your dollars, then it pays to be patient and wait until *after* your baby shower to pick up any final items you've been considering.
15. *Network with other parents.* Parents can be a great resource for learning about sales and promotions in your area. Form a network or neighborhood tribe and share the latest deals.

Financially Preparing to be a Stay-at-Home Parent

There are plenty of practical and personal benefits to becoming a stay-at-home parent. Financially, you will save money on childcare, and emotionally, you'll be able to spend quality time with your little one. But most stay-at-home parents that I've interviewed have said they were only able to leave their jobs and take the plunge after making serious sacrifices to their budget.

To help ease your transition, follow these guidelines if you're considering becoming a stay-at-home parent.

Make sure you're both onboard. Being a stay-at-home parent is most certainly a team effort. Both you and your spouse need to be ready for this transition.

Carefully review your finances. You can't go into this with blinders on. Otherwise, the change will be overly stressful and cause tension in your marriage. Have a money date and review your numbers. See where you're at today and what changes would be needed in order for one of you to become a stay-at-home parent.

Make sure essentials are covered by only one income. You don't have to wait until you have children to do this step. In fact, I think that all couples should adopt this mindset, and that is why I developed the Couple Money budget around this goal. (Refer to Chapter Three if you need a refresher.)

Do a test run. Begin living off of one income as soon as possible. See firsthand if this is a viable solution for your family by actually putting it into practice.

It helps to be debt free. My general advice is to become debt free if you want to be a stay-at-home parent. Or, at the very least, make sure that you've paid off your high interest loans before quitting your job. Otherwise, you could be harming your finances and putting your family's financial well-being at risk.

Be willing to adjust. Being parents doesn't change the fact that life happens, so understand that it will take constant adjustments to make your budget work. I see plenty of money dates in your future!

CHAPTER 12

Financially Preparing for Homeownership

Owning your own home is a dream for many, but it can often feel like an unattainable goal. There just doesn't seem to be enough money in the budget to cover the monthly expenses that come with homeownership, and saving enough for a down payment seems downright impossible. But if you're willing to put in the legwork and develop your financial plan, then you'll be able to reach your goal of becoming a homeowner much sooner than you think.

If you're new to the homebuying process, follow the six steps provided to help ensure that you're making a smart financial and emotional decision.

Step 1: Know Your Debt-to-Income Ratio

I will say up front that I don't think home ownership is for everyone. If you currently have a high amount of debt, then you should think twice about applying for a mortgage. It will only compound your problems and make it that much harder to pay off your existing debts. If you're unsure whether you're currently carrying too much debt to sensibly think about buying a home, review your debt-to-income ratio.

To calculate this ratio, simply add up all of your debt (student loans, credit cards, car loans, etc.) and divide that amount by your total income. At the very least, your debt-to-income ratio should be less than 36 percent. Anything above that will make it difficult, if not impossible, to qualify for a mortgage.

Step 2: Don't Forget Your Other Goals!

It's easy to become blinded by the goal of buying and owning your first home. Between going to open houses and talking to realtors and lenders, it's easy to get caught up in the moment. But don't forget about your other goals, too! Just because you'd like to buy a home, it doesn't mean that you can stop saving for retirement or put off paying down your student loans. To remind yourself about the importance of your other goals, ask yourselves the following two questions. If you answer "no" to either of these, you should rethink your goal of homeownership.

1. After purchasing our new home, will we still be able to save for retirement?
2. Can we afford the down payment and monthly housing costs without dipping into our emergency fund?

Step 3: Consider Your Down Payment Amount

Aim big when you're figuring out your down payment amount. The advantage of a larger down payment is that it will reduce your monthly mortgage bill, and it may even reduce your interest rate. If you put down 20 percent or more, you can avoid having to pay private mortgage insurance (PMI), too. Talk to your lender to see how your down payment amount will affect your mortgage, and make sure that he or she is willing to hold your hand through the entire loan process.

If you're having difficulty saving enough money to make a 20 percent down payment, then you may want to hold off purchasing a home for the time being.

Location	Average 20% Down	Location	Average 20% Down
San Francisco, CA	$153,600	Phoenix, AZ	$42,060
Los Angeles, CA	$109,580	Philadelphia, PA	$40,360
San Diego, CA	$97,600	Las Vegas, NV	$38,920
Boston, MA	$76,220	Chicago, IL	$38,200
Seattle, WA	$71,880	Houston, TX	$33,400
Washington, D.C.	$71,060	Atlanta, GA	$32,800
Denver, CO	$62,760	Columbus, OH	$29,920
Portland, OR	$60,180	St. Louis, MO	$27,270
Baltimore, MD	$47,840	Indianapolis, IN	$25,700
Miami, FL	$44,680	Pittsburgh, PA	$25,080
Minneapolis, MN	$42,740	*National Average*	*$36,500*

Step 4: Understand the True Cost of Homeownership

When figuring out how much home you can afford, keep in mind that there are additional expenses besides your mortgage that you'll be responsible for.

Lenders typically focus on the actual mortgage payments that you'll be making, and it will be up to you to factor in other housing costs like utilities, maintenance, lawn care, furnishings, and a house emergency fund.

If your potential neighborhood has a homeowners association (HOA), look not only at this year's fee, but review previous years as well. You may find that the HOA fee rises considerably year after year.

In addition to these ongoing expenses, remember to factor in one-time expenses, too, like moving costs, new appliances, and the cost to buy out the remainder of your lease if you were renting.

Step 5: Consider the Resale Value

Unless you're moving into your forever home, you should think about the possibility that someday you'll need to sell the property. When that day comes, you need to make sure that you'll at least get your money back (and maybe even turn a profit). Although this is probably the furthest thing from your mind today, considering the future resale potential now will pay off down the road. Aside from the financial factors already discussed, consider these additional questions that will affect the resale value.

- What's the quality of the general public services in the community?
- Are there available recreation facilities nearby?
- What's the quality of the local public school system?
- What are the latest crime statistics for the community?
- What's the overall quality of life in the community?

Step 6: Get a Home Inspection!

Once you've found the home of your dreams and double checked your finances, the next step is to schedule a home inspection. One of the smartest moves you can make during the homebuying process is hiring a top-notch inspector. While a great real estate agent can help you find a beautiful home, a great inspector will help make sure you're not buying a lemon. Don't underestimate the peace of mind that comes from a thorough home inspection.

Why Home Inspections Are So Important

Take it from an experienced homeowner, there are few things that can drain your wallet faster than extensive (and expensive) home repairs. That's why home inspections are crucial. They are designed to protect you, the buyer, in what will probably be the biggest purchase of your life.

A well-trained home inspector will evaluate your potential house in great detail. They will look at the structure and mechanical systems, and identify anything that needs to be repaired or replaced.

What to Expect During a Home Inspection

If you're a first-time homebuyer, you may be wondering how exactly a home inspection works. While it can vary somewhat depending on the condition of the house, there are general guidelines that have to be followed by all licensed inspectors.

Expect that your home inspection will take several hours. This gives your inspector plenty of time to look over the house from top to bottom and dig deeper into any potential problems that he or she may find.

A proper inspection is a detailed process where the inspector reviews all of the following:

- The exterior, including windows, siding, gutters, decks, and walkways.
- The roof, including the materials, drainage system, and chimney (if applicable).
- The structure of the home, including walls, floors, and foundations.
- Heating and cooling systems, including the furnace, duct-work, and central air.
- All plumbing, including the toilets, sinks, and faucets.
- All electrical work, including the wiring, central panel, and sub-panels.

Please keep in mind that cosmetic work doesn't fall under the home inspector's responsibilities. The inspector's focus is on the function of your potential home, not the curb appeal.

It's important that you try to be present for the home inspection. Besides gaining a better understanding of the home from an unbiased professional, you can also ask questions and receive honest feedback about the condition of the home.

Soon after the physical inspection is complete, you'll receive a written report from the home inspector. If there's any information included in the report that you don't understand, be sure to ask. Once you receive the report, review it will your realtor and determine if the problem items should be fixed by the seller, or if your offer price should be lowered so that you can make the repairs on your own.

Step 7: Understand Your Mortgage

Before you sign on the dotted line and officially make the biggest purchase of your lifetime, make sure that you understand all of the legal and financial terms found in your mortgage. This means becoming familiar with mortgage-related jargon, as well.

Below are answers to the most common mortgage-related questions that are asked by first-time homebuyers. This is meant to give you give you a better understanding of your mortgage and the fine-print involved.

Which type of mortgage is best, fixed-rate or ARM?

In general, you should avoid adjustable rate mortgages (ARMs) because the interest rates will change over the life of the mortgage depending on market conditions. The problem with ARMs is that borrowers don't know what their interest rate will adjust to until it's often too late to lock in a better rate. This was partially responsible for the housing crisis in the late 2000s. Fixed rate mortgages, on the other hand, are considered safer because they allow borrowers to lock in interest rates that never change.

Is my APR the same as my interest rate?

APR stands for annual percentage rate, and it's a tool used to standardize the comparison between mortgages. It's the annualized cost of the mortgage, including the interest and lender's fees. The Consumer Financial Protection Bureau (CFPB) recommends that borrowers always use APR when comparing different loans.

The interest rate is a component of APR, but it only takes into account the interest charged on the mortgage and ignores all other fees.

What are origination fees?

Origination fees cover a variety of services provided by the lender when preparing a mortgage. These fees generally range from 0.5 to 1 percent of the total loan amount and vary by lender.

What are "points" and how do they work?

Points are essentially prepaid interest, and they're used to buy down the interest rate on a mortgage. For example, a $200,000 mortgage may carry a 5% interest rate. However, if you buy two points at closing ($4,000), then your interest rate may drop to 4.75%.

CHAPTER 13

How to Retire Early

I've had the privilege of interviewing several couples on my podcast who have been able to retire early. Most of the time, their original goal wasn't to actually retire early at all. Instead they just wanted to save enough money to quit working, travel more, or spend more time with their family. But as I kept interviewing these couples, I noticed that common patterns would emerge. There seemed to be two keys to success that allowed these couples to not only achieve their financial goals, but to retire early, too. Those patterns were their ability to resist lifestyle inflation, and their willingness to embrace a frugal lifestyle.

Resisting Lifestyle Inflation

Sometimes we can be our own worst enemies when it comes to managing our finances. This is especially true when our income increases through a pay raise or windfall, and our expenses seem to keep pace and increase, too. While some level of lifestyle inflation may be justified (buying better quality items may mean paying more upfront), it can also be a sign that we're unable to balance our needs and our wants.

For example, if you receive a raise at work, does that mean you really *need* to buy a new car? If you receive a promotion and you'd like to upgrade your living conditions, do you *need* to build a new custom home with all the bells and whistles? Separating your needs from your wants will allow you to bank your increased earnings, and that, in turn, will allow you to shave years off your retirement date.

Embracing the Frugal Lifestyle

I believe that being frugal is an essential tool to building wealth. In fact, finding ways to decrease your nonessential expenses can be a great use of your time. In addition to improving your bottom line and allowing you to retire sooner, it also simplifies your life and reduces stress. By no longer worrying about "keep up with the Joneses," you'll have more time to focus on what really matters.

Make no mistake, being frugal is a lifestyle. It's not just brown-bagging your lunch a few days each week. It's a mindset that encompasses your entire financial life. To embrace the frugal lifestyle, you need to find a "why" that is bigger than yourself. For example, some couples that I've talked to said they became frugal so they could have more resources to help others. Others said it allowed them to cut back their hours at work so they could volunteer more and make a difference in their community. Regardless of the reason, make sure that you review your motivation for going frugal to make sure it's sustainable.

The Secret to Retiring Early

If you want to retire early, you're going to need to save more than the standard 5 to 10 percent of your income that you may have been doing up to this point. To truly build wealth and put yourself in a position where you can retire early and live off your investments, you're going to need to save at least 30 percent of your annul income. It sounds like a lot, but it's not impossible. Consider these tips to start increasing your savings percentage today.

Become a one-car household. If your work situation and lifestyle allow for it, consider selling your second car and becoming a one-car household. I know this might be a drastic step that isn't practical for everyone, but if you want to do something radical like retire in your 50s (or sooner) then you need to think big. Having only one car will lower your cost of gas, insurance, maintenance, and repairs.

Reconsider where you live. Your geographic location has a significant impact on how far your money will go. Moving to an area where the cost of living is cheaper will allow you to grow your retirement fund and retire sooner. If you're not ready to leave the city, consider moving to a different neighborhood that is still up and coming, or that will reduce your need for two cars.

Review your monthly bills. As part of your routine budget planning, you should always review your bills and look for ways to cut back. I was recently able to lower my internet bill by 15 percent by making a single phone call. You'll need a combination of these small wins along with the big ones if you want to retire early.

Develop a system to fight lifestyle inflation. Having a system in place to regularly review your expenses will help you fight against lifestyle inflation. Your money dates are the perfect time to do this!

Learn from others. I suggest soaking up as much information as you can from those who have already reached the finish line. Two wonderful sites to visit are *Mr. Money Mustache* and *Root of Good*. On *Mr. Money Mustache*, Pete Adeney shares how he was able to comfortably retire at age 30, and on *Root of Good*, Justin explains how he managed to retire at age 33! Each site provides a number of helpful tips that will help guide you to becoming financially independent at an early age.

Is a "Hybrid Retirement" Right for You?

What does the idea of retiring mean to you? Does it mean truly "retiring"—putting your feet up on the beach and never looking at another spreadsheet again? Or is your concept of retirement different? I know plenty of people who shudder to think what will happen when they look at their calendars and see them blank for the first time ever. If you're in this camp, then retiring might mean quitting your nine-to-five job and exploring a new business venture, or investing in real estate, etc., instead. You're not officially "retiring" by traditional standards, but rather you're allowing yourself to give full attention to doing what you love, rather than what you have to do to pay your bills. That freedom is what retiring means to many of us.

If this idea of a hybrid or stepping-stone retirement interests you, then explore the option further over a money date. Perhaps you can set a goal of building a second income stream that will allow you to quit your full-time jobs and explore your options. Or, at the very least, discuss how you would spend your 30s, 40s, 50, and beyond if you were able to retire early, and build the conversation from there.

Find Your Retirement Number

Now that you have a picture of what you want your retirement to look like, it's time to figure out how much money you'll need to get there. Even though every couple is different, we can start with a few general assumptions:

1. You want to be able to live off your retirement income and investment portfolio.
2. You want your money to last through retirement.

To determine how much money you'll need, we'll be using the safe withdrawal rate strategy. Basically, your safe withdrawal rate is the maximum amount that you can withdraw from your accounts each year without depleting your nest egg. I'll be using 4 percent as the rate. To put this into practice, take your annual spending and multiply by 25.

- If you're spending $35,000 per year, then you'll need to save $875,000 in order to retire.
- If you're spending $70,000 per year, then you'll need to save $1,750,000 in order to retire.
- If you're spending $125,000 per year, then you'll need to save $3,125,000 in order to retire.

As you can see, lowering your annual expenses has a significant impact on your nest egg. Is the 4 percent withdrawal rate a one-size-fits-all solution? No, but it's a practical starting point. If you want to be more conservative, consider reducing the rate to 3 percent, but this will increase your savings requirement by an additional 25 percent.

In addition to using the safe withdrawal rate strategy, I also recommend referring to the following chart which allows you to further customize your retirement needs based on the length of your retirement and your estimated investment return.

Income Need	Length of Retirement	4% Return	6% Return	8% Return
$25,000	10 years	$239,455	$220,448	$203,853
$25,000	20 years	$456,857	$385,880	$330,751
$25,000	30 years	$654,237	$510,027	$409,744
$35,000	10 years	$335,238	$308,628	$285,395
$35,000	20 years	$639,600	$540,233	$463,052
$35,000	30 years	$915,932	$714,038	$573,642
$50,000	10 years	$478,911	$440,897	$407,707
$50,000	20 years	$913,715	$771,761	$661,502
$50,000	30 years	$1,308,474	$1,020,054	$819,488
$65,000	10 years	$622,584	$573,166	$530,019
$65,000	20 years	$1,187,829	$1,003,290	$859,952
$65,000	30 years	$1,701,017	$1,326,070	$1,065,334
$75,000	10 years	$718,366	$661,345	$611,560
$75,000	20 years	$1,370,572	$1,157,641	$992,263
$75,000	30 years	$1,962,711	$1,530,081	$1,229,232

If you've found your retirement number and you're feeling discouraged, don't be! You're making your first pass at your retirement projection and you're planning for your future—that should be celebrated! And now you have a benchmark that you can use to track your progress from this point forward. Remember, your deficit will only get smaller as you continue using the principles outlined in this book.

Parting Thoughts

Congrats on finishing the four-week program! Even though this is the end of the book, I hope this is the beginning of an incredible marriage filled with happiness and love. Building your marriage and wealth is more than just numbers; it's about working together as a team to achieve your dreams.

By the way, if you haven't already, drop me a line and let me know the incredible things the two of you are doing together. You can reach me at hello@couplemoney.com. I'd love to hear from you!

APPENDIX

———◆◆———

10 Resources to Build Your Marriage and Wealth

I started *Couple Money* because I wanted to provide a safe space to discuss not only finances, but also the very deeply personal parts of marriage. When I began, there weren't many platforms that dove into both sides, but today there are plenty of wonderful sites and podcasts dedicated to these topics. Each has their own unique take on relationships and money, and I'm sure if you explore them you'll find some new favorites, too.

- *His & Her Money.* Tai and Talaat McNeely share their story of falling in love, getting married, and discovering they were total opposites when it came to managing their finances. With their blog, they invite you into their home and personal lives, and show you how they managed to climb out of debt not once, but twice, together.
- *One Extraordinary Marriage.* Tony and Alisa DiLorenzo focus on intimacy, whether it's emotional, financial, or physical. They're committed to being open and frank about their marriage, and they provide practical tips to help you and your spouse become more connected.
- *Marriage, Kids and Money.* Andy Hill is focused on taking care of his family and providing them with the best

lives possible. He shares his quest to become debt free, as well as his plan to pay off his mortgage by the end of the year. An impressive feat considering Andy is only thirty-five years old!

- *The Smart Couple.* Jayson Gaddis has created a resource to help couples have deeper conversations and more meaningful connections. He will teach you how to use conflict to create fulfilling and sustainable relationships through his virtual relationship empowerment classes.

- *Family Balance Sheet.* Kristia's site shares personal stories, practical tips, and delicious recipes to help your busy family live well for less. If you're looking for motivation to become debt free, check out her series!

- *The Budget Mama.* After failing with money in her early adult life, Jessie Fearon set out to conquer her finances and experience financial freedom. On her site, she shares her family's real life on a budget with the hope of encouraging you to realize your dreams.

- *Mom and Dad Money.* Matt Beck is a fee-only financial planner who started his site to help new parents build happy families by making money simple. His mission is to provide new parents with down-to-earth financial advice specifically tailored to their unique situation.

- *Engaged Marriage.* Dustin and Bethany Riechmann provide practical tips, tools, and training to help busy married couples overcome financial and romantic issues to live a life they love. Their goal is to help keep marriages fresh and fully engaged, even when life gets hectic.

- *Confessions of a Terrible Husband.* As you can guess from the title, Nick Pavlidis has no qualms about getting into the messy realities of marriage. His site is committed to inspiring, encouraging, and equipping you to improve your marriage.

- *Order of Man.* Ryan Michler believes that most, if not all, of the world's biggest problems could be solved if males everywhere learned how to be better husbands, fathers, friends, and leaders. He's on a mission to help all men realize their full potential.

52 Fun and Frugal Date Ideas

Not all dates need to be elaborate or expensive to be memorable. In fact, the simplest dates are often the ones that leave the most lasting impression. Here's a collection of easy, frugal, and fun date ideas that you can enjoy together for an entire year (and beyond)!

Explore Local Spots

1. *Visit historic landmarks.* Learn about your local history—and take the time to read the plaques, too!
2. *Tour a brewery.* Find a local brewery in your area using www.BreweryMap.com and take a tour. Once you're finished, compare notes over a couple of pints.
3. *Enjoy a concert.* Local bands can offer a great bang for your buck and provide an intimate and enjoyable experience.
4. *Enjoy a ferry ride.* Ferry rides can be a relaxing way to spend a lazy afternoon. Plus you'll get to see your city from a new point of view.
5. *Visit a farmers' market.* Eat local and have some fun at the farmers' market. And the best part? You'll be supporting your local community, too.
6. *Appreciate the architecture.* Go downtown and take an architectural tour. Snap pics of your favorite designs.

7. *Get a bird's eye view.* Sometimes a new perspective can be fun. Relax on the rooftop of a high rise and watch the city below.

8. *Take in a ballgame.* See if there are any minor league ballgames in your area. Tickets are less expensive than the pros and you can get much closer to the action.

9. *Check out a local festival.* Check your community calendar and visit a nearby festival.

10. *Indulge in some campus fun.* Local colleges can be a great source of talent. See a campus production of a play or concert.

11. *Try a new restaurant.* Check Groupon for deals and try a new local restaurant. You might just discover your new favorite spot!

Enjoy Nature

12. *Go for a hike.* Visit a local park and take a relaxing walk (or a strenuous hike if you're feeling adventurous).

13. *Have a picnic.* Take advantage of the pleasant weather and have a lunch or dinner date outside.

14. *Build a sandcastle.* Those living by the beach have a great spot for a date. Too easy!

15. *Go fishing.* See who can catch the most fish, or just spend the day relaxing and chatting.

16. *Build and fly a kite.* Be a kid again and fly a kite. Or better yet, grab a kit and build one from scratch.

17. *Count the stars.* Pick a clear night and look for constellations.

18. *Go bird watching.* See how many local birds you can identify using an app like iBird Pro or BirdsEye.

19. *Visit the botanical gardens.* If you're looking to catch up with each other in beautiful surroundings, visit your local botanical gardens for your next leisurely stroll.

20. *Tour a vineyard.* Take a drive to a nearby vineyard and enjoy a tour of their grounds.

21. *Plant a garden.* Plant flowers or grow your own herbs and veggies in your backyard.

Play Games & Get Fit

22. *Go bowling.* Grab a lane and see who can break 100 the fastest.

23. *Bike around the city.* Discover the nooks and crannies of your town with a bike tour.

24. *Play tennis.* Play against each other or ask another couple to join in the fun and play doubles.

25. *Go mini-golfing.* Playing putt-putt can be a casual way to relax and enjoy the outdoors.

26. *Run your neighborhood.* Get in shape and have a race to a neighborhood coffee or pastry shop.

27. *Go for a swim.* There's no better way to cool down in the summer.

28. *Take a dance class.* Learn new moves at your local dance studio or rent a DVD from the library so you can practice at home.

29. *Go on a treasure hunt.* Mix it up and hide some items around your neighborhood, leaving clues for your spouse to find them.

30. *Throw the frisbee.* Strapped for cash, but still want to enjoy nature? Pick up a frisbee and head to your local park.

31. *Train for a 5k.* My husband and I tried this one, and believe me, the weeks fly by!

All the World Is a Stage

32. *Give stand-up comedy a try.* Take advantage of open mic night and get your husband or wife laughing.
33. *Sing karaoke.* Bare your soul with a tune. Extra points if you sing something special like your wedding song or something related to your first date.
34. *Create sidewalk art.* Grab some sidewalk chalk and create art to let each other know how you feel.
35. *Paint a picture.* Take an art class and paint a picture for each other.
36. *Write poetry.* Write and share a poem that you've created for your spouse.

Dream Together

37. *Plan a trip together.* Spend a day virtually exploring a new city and come up with places you'd love to visit in person.
38. *Go house hunting.* Visit a neighborhood where you'd love to live and attend a few open houses. You can get a better idea of how much your dream home will cost you, too!
39. *Start a band.* Learn a new instrument or brush up on an old one. Record a song together.
40. *Volunteer.* Pick a charity that you both support and spend the day helping others.
41. *Create a vision board.* Looking to explore your future? Make a vision board and dream big!

42. *Start a blog.* Seriously, this can be fun if you have a shared interest that you'd love to explore together.

Enjoy an Evening In

43. *Try a family recipe.* Each of you make a special dish from your side of the family. Bon appétit!
44. *Have a nostalgia movie night.* Already seen each other's favorite movies? Why not watch a favorite one from your childhood instead!
45. *Take a look, it's in a book.* (I'm a Reading Rainbow kid if you can't tell...) Create a book club for two. You can have quiet reading sessions and then come together to discuss the latest chapter.
46. *Learn a new skill.* Are you both interested in painting or photography? Go online and develop a new skill together.
47. *Tackle a home project.* Check out your local hardware store for classes and ideas.
48. *Scrapbook.* Grab your pictures and spend the weekend putting together a scrapbook of your memories.
49. *Binge-watch a new show.* Weather not cooperating? Stay home and discover a new series.
50. *Write a script.* If you're film buffs or enjoy writing, try your hand at a movie script. Even if it never becomes a blockbuster, you'll have created a story that you both love.
51. *Plant a memory.* Planting a tree and watching it grow together can be a beautiful way to reminisce through the years.
52. *Homebrew together.* Make your own beers and meads, and then celebrate your creation with friends.

ABOUT THE AUTHOR

Elle Martinez is the creator and award-winning blogger behind *Couple Money*, a site and podcast dedicated to helping spouses build their marriage and wealth together.

Each week she interviews financial experts and real-life couples who've achieved impressive financial goals like becoming debt free, starting a business, and retiring early. Through her podcast, she finds patterns and habits that help couples become successful.

In addition to *Couple Money*, Elle has been a contributing writer to such major media platforms as *Business Insider*, *TurboTax*, *Entrepreneur*, *Lending Tree*, and many more. Connect with Elle on Twitter @couplemoney, and visit her website www.couplemoney.com for the latest tips on money and marriage.

INDEX

Insurance discounts, 92-93

Insurance premium, 47, 90-94

Insurance specialist, 95

Interest rate, 32-33, 43-44, 99-100, 102, 125, 129-130

International stock market, 84

Internship, 29

Investing mistakes, 86-87

Investing now vs. investing later, 80

Investment advisor, 87-88

Investment portfolio, 79, 135

iPod, 60, 65

IRA, 82-83

IRS, 81-82

J - L

Jetta, 56

Job loss, 30

Joint account, 41-42, 45-46

Joint vs. separate accounts, 41-42

Kayak, 110

Large-cap mutual fund, 84

Lawn care, 125

Lending Tree, 147

Liabilities, 15-17, 50

Life insurance, 82, 90-91

Lifecycle fund, 85

Lifestyle inflation, 131-132

Living expenses, 29, 56

Loaded mutual fund, 83-84

Loan-to-value ratio, 102

M

Maintenance fee, 43

Market timing, 86

Marriage, Kids and Money, 139-140

Married Food, 120

McNeely, Tai, 139

McNeely, Talaat, 139

Michler, Ryan, 141

Mid-cap mutual fund, 84

Mint, 16, 26

Mom and Dad Money, 140

Money date, 3-9, 12-13, 17-20, 28, 35-39, 49-51, 121-122, 133-134

Money date checklist, 5-6

Money market account, 44

Mortgage, 16, 44, 47, 98-100, 123-125, 129-130, 140

Made in United States
Troutdale, OR
01/10/2025

27824520R00096